Praise for Cathy's Books

Snowflake from the Hand of God

In this book, Cathy Cash Spellman reaches into the deepest recesses of the human heart and returns with great insight in managing the challenges of life. Beauty, compassion, and wisdom are the hallmarks of these pages.

Larry Dossey, M.D.
Author: *Healing Beyond the Body*,
Reinventing Medicine and *Healing Words*

Lark's Labyrinth

The author constructs a blistering story–replete with political and religious intrigue–that never slows down and will keep readers turning the pages of this spectacular thrill ride. An absolute must for Spellman fans."

-*Publisher's Weekly*

Paint the Wind

"Paint the Wind is the Gone with the Wind of the West."
- *Gerald A. Browne, author of 11 Harrowhouse.*

So Many Partings

"Almost impossible to put down. Cathy Cash Spellman has the ability to produce one powerful scene after another, and the strong plotting draws you helplessly on."

- *Publishers Weekly*

"A cross between The Thorn Birds and Ragtime!"
– *New York Daily News*

The Message

Cathy Cash Spellman

This book is about
a channeled experience

The Wild Harp & Company, Incorporated

© 2014 The Wild Harp & Company, Inc.

All Rights Reserved. No part of this book may be reproduced or transmitted in any form or by any means, graphic, electronic, or mechanical, including photocopying, recording, taping, or by any information storage or retrieval system, without prior permission in writing from the Author.

The Wild Harp & Company,
Incorporated
Westport, CT 06880

www.CathyCashSpellman.com

ISBN: 978-0615974965

Dedication

This book is for Dakota – no words on earth could describe my love for you or my joy in being your Mother.

Novels by Cathy Cash Spellman

So Many Partings
An Excess of Love
Paint the Wind
Bless the Child
The Playground of the Gods
Lark's Labyrinth

Non-fiction

Notes to My Daughters

Philosophy & Poetry

Snowflake from the Hand of God

Table of Contents

Part I – The Message		1
Chapter 1	Vega	3
Chapter 2	The Message Begins	9
Chapter 3	Reincarnation	15
Chapter 4	Work on My Body	19
Chapter 5	Gaia	23
Chapter 6	The Deer	29
Part II – Planetary Dangers		35
Chapter 7	The Rape of the Planet & our Food Supply	37
Chapter 8	True History of the Planet Earth	51
Chapter 9	Creation	83
Part III – My Life with the Unseen		89
Chapter 10	Oneness of Creation	91
Part IV – Cleveland on Tuesday		95
Chapter 11	Free Will	97
Chapter 12	Humanity and Free Will	101
Chapter 13	The DNA of Humans	105
Chapter 14	Manipulation of Truth	111
Chapter 15	Love. The Heart of the Matter	119
Chapter 16	Love/Sex/Relationship	123
Chapter 17	The Other Side of Love… Women and Divorce	127
Chapter 18	Love Vibration	131
Chapter 19	Heart Teaching	137
Chapter 20	Sexuality	141
Chapter 21	The Nature of Time	143
Chapter 22	Essence of Time	145
Part V – Conclusion, It's Not Too Late		153

Foreword

The Message was channeled to me over several years, starting in the middle nineties. At the time I was deeply engaged in serious spiritual pursuits – healing, shamanic journeying, martial arts and mystical research were occupying large amounts of my time and consciousness. I believe that when we open the psychic portals through ceremony, ritual and serious study, we gain access to other realms from those our ordinary consciousness permits.

I have no way of proving the authenticity of the Message I received, but I was deeply touched by what was said and have always wanted to share it with any who wish to know of its existence. It has circulated among close friends who've encouraged me to open it to a wider audience now because so much of what The Message prophesied and explained seems to be unfolding now.

In channeling, messages are received, but their origin can never be proven. Are they from the Cosmos, the Collective Unconscious of humanity or from our own fertile imagination and heart? Nobody knows for certain – least of all those who receive the transmissions, so I can only say I'm sincere in my belief that the experience was real and that The Mothers, whose message it is, give voice to the female essence of God.

I leave it to you, dear Reader, to decide for yourself if this is Divinely inspired Truth or allegory. If the Message rings true for you, as it does so clearly for me, perhaps that's all that really matters.

Cathy Cash Spellman

Prologue

I want to share with you the experience of receiving information from a source I can't name and can't prove. I do this with some reluctance, as I don't relish the idea of making myself vulnerable by revelation, but because the message is important, especially in these precarious times, I don't believe I should keep it to myself. I've learned beyond doubt that we're all in this life together. When Jesus said, "Love God, love your fellow man – this is the whole of the law," I believe He was providing us with the simple rulebook for the game of life.

I also think the game is going into overtime, and there's a possibility some of the information I've received could be helpful to any who care to use it – if only to reinforce their own intuitive sense of truth. I don't wish to proselytize in any way about this message. The best I can do is tell you what I was told and let you decide if it has any validity in your life.

I've been told that those who have ears to hear will hear and eyes to see will see, and I've been given the job of messenger. The rest is in the hands of Those whose message it really is.

A Message to the Heart of the World

I call them The Mothers. Three female voices of Deity from three different cultures all with the same message. They say it doesn't matter how we name them – Mary, Isis, Gaia, Sipi Gualmo – they've been called by a 1,000 names in as many places and timeslots. Being eternal has its perks.

Over a period of several years they gave me information they said was a message from the female Heart of God to the heart of the world. What's in this small book is just a fraction of what they had to say. It began for me in 1998, and by now so many things they spoke of have happened, I feel guilty about not having shared the message earlier with other than close friends and family. But, in truth, I thought no one would believe me – mass food and water poisoning, widespread hunger and poverty, threat of revolution – all these things seemed implausible in the euphoric 90's. I didn't know what to make of having been given this material, and I didn't know how to circulate its wisdom to a wider world.

I was wary of both the information and its source when these transmissions began, but over the years of receiving the words each day and of working with the energies I was shown, I came to believe the experience was real and that the Mothers are the female essence of God revealing themselves to us in a time when humanity gravely needs a Mother's love.

A few of the topics the Mothers have talked about include:

- The True History of Earth
- A Hybrid Race
- The Future of the Planet
- The Coming Hard Times
- What on Earth is Wrong?
- How to Fix It
- The Nature of Time
- Reincarnation
- What is God/Goddess?
- Energy
- Love and Sex
- A Woman-centric Time in the Making

- The Oneness of Creation
- Religion and Spirit
- Belief Systems
- Joy
- How to Heal the Heart and the Body

PART I
The Message

CHAPTER 1

Vega

The Message began in the middle to late '90s. I had been doing sacred ceremonial work with Shamans and Native American medicine men for several years and I was Irish, so Second Sight was not an unknown phenomenon for me. I was aware of communication from other realms of consciousness, but at the moment this channeling of The Message began nothing could have been farther from my mind.

I was being worked on by Dr. John Upledger at the Upledger Institute, and as I lay on his examining table (as I had often done before), I became aware of a shaft of brilliant white Light that had somehow entered the healing room. Everything around me faded into unimportance, and I perceived, standing in the center of the Light, an imposing figure dressed in a long white robe. He was not ethereal as an angel, but seemed

nearly corporeal, almost as if I could reach out and touch him. He was quite tall, had a very serious demeanor and enormous dignity. I was
so startled, I blurted out to John what I was seeing, and he had the presence of mind to suggest I ask the Being his name. He said he could see the brilliant shaft of light, too, but couldn't discern what was inside it.

The entity said he was called Vega and told me not to be alarmed. He said he'd been sent to take the place of the spiritual guardians I usually rely on, for a period of one year, which would be the most significant of my life. During the next twelve months of rigorous training, he said, he would be my only guide.

I didn't like the sound of that. I relied on my usual spiritual Guides, and trusted them. I'd been raised a Catholic and had studied many comparative Theologies over the years, so I was no stranger to the notion of saints and angels guiding the affairs of humans, but this was different and it was happening to *me*, not to St. Therese of Avila.

For more than 20 years I'd been a serious student and practitioner of a number of hands-on healing modalities, including Chinese Medicine. I'd learned that most healers are aware of considerable "other worldly" help that comes to them in the healing room – guides and angels, spirit doctors if you will, whose job it is to help those who seek to help others. For that matter, I know many conventional medical doctors who would probably say much the same thing. My own such Guides and angels are stalwart and kindly and I trust them.

Vega seemed authoritative and of a very different stripe. Why should I trust him? I asked myself...and why would those I'd so long relied on in spirit have consigned me to a stranger's care without warning me?

Vega held up his hand to shortcut the torrent of questions I was about to spew. He was calm and deliberate. "You have come into this incarnation carrying a heavy burden of sorrow in your cellular makeup," he said gravely. "You've been killed in many lifetimes for speaking truth in the service of the Celestials. In this lifetime you will not die for your truth, but will speak it aloud to multitudes." He didn't let me in on exactly *what* that truth would be. But he did add that I was here as well, to make the way clear for another truth-speaker, one who would carry the divine gift of not being misunderstood by any who heard the message.

As he spoke, the Light around him intensified to a blinding brilliance. He told me great teachers – earthly ones – had already been sent throughout my lifetime, both to instruct me and to clear the sorrow from my lungs, where it lurked on an energetic level.

"The residual understanding of suffering that your past life experiences have imparted to you," he said "is essential to the task that lies ahead. Difficult times are coming for humanity. Times when the primary healing available to much of humankind will be empathetic energy work. Those who have deeply experienced the frequency of sorrow and suffering will empathically tune in to the needy – both individual and planetary – and they will have the power to heal by transmitting this vibration in a manner you have yet to learn."

He raised his hand and passed it over my eyes. A reprise of future images flashed in front of me like pictures in a Nickelodeon. I saw myself and others, in some future moment, in a time of hardship and decimation, working on people in a way I'd never before seen. I was shocked, awestruck and very, very disturbed by the vision.

Vega smiled gently, obviously having read my mind. "There will be joy as well," he offered, "to balance the scales of your life. And what you have seen is but one possible timeline. There may yet be time to alter it."

I was quite shaken by the vision. Even joy in a ravaged world sounded dicey. I asked what was expected of me.

"You must meditate at dawn and dusk daily," he said, "and write down every word that is said. All will be made clear to you as time goes on. Your psychic channeling gift is most powerful at these times of day and the energies are clearest for our purpose."

Vega then told me in a straightforward way, replete with mind-blowing visions, about my past and *future* life. Most of what he said and showed was far too intimate for any earthly source to know. The more accurate his knowledge of me seemed to be, the more distressed I became. The visions ended. The light faded. Vega made a sign that I took to be one of blessing and then he, too, vanished. I lay on the table for some time, tears running down my cheeks, trying to process all I'd seen and heard.

Finally, I sat up and looked at John, who shook his head as if to say, "Who knows?" We both knew something profound had taken place. John had always admonished me not to seek to know too much about the secrets of the Universe, but rather to let whatever knowledge I'm supposed to have unfold in its own good time. Could this strange experience be part of such unfoldment, or was it something else entirely?

John said he'd been monitoring my body's responses during the interchange and he could feel the authenticity of the experience by the way in which my body had behaved while I was speaking with the entity. He said he wished he'd been able to see the Being, not just the Light, and asked if I thought the name Vega meant the entity might be from the distant star of the same name. I said I didn't have a clue.

We hugged and parted company. I promised to let him know if anything further developed.

I went back to the hotel with the intention of going to the beach to clear my head and forget those disturbing visions. But once you're touched by fate, nothing is ever the same again. Rosalyn Bruyere, a friend of mine who is a major mystic and healer, always says that being in God's army is like joining the Mob, except that you can't die and get out. That's how I felt that day, walking on the beach and staring at the ocean: as if I'd just been drafted into some Army and been given sealed orders.

The sky was gray and the wind so strong the beach had been closed to swimmers. The late afternoon tableau is still a perfect picture in my mind, yet underneath the perfection, was the niggling fear that I'd turned a corner and wandered into alien territory, with no certainty of where the road would lead.

CHAPTER 2

The Message Begins

I headed home troubled about the disturbing experience, yet seriously considering doing what I'd been told to do, mostly out of curiosity. I'd done sacred ceremonial work for years with mystics and shamans who regularly talked to disembodied visitors. My Mother's family was well-known in its part of Ireland for its psychic gifts. I knew such communication wasn't impossible. The conversation with Vega, whoever he was, had been too unsettling for me not to want to know more. I didn't really believe Vega was extraterrestrial, maybe because I found that too scary. Not that I doubted the existence of other life in the Universe – it seemed ridiculously arrogant to think we were the only intelligent beings God ever made – but, the thought of aliens frightened me and I'd steered away from poking into anything about them during my years of psychic investigation.

Nonetheless, I began to get up at 4:30 a.m. each day to pray and to channel. For a while, I tried to do the same at dusk, but that was considerably harder.

I didn't really know the correct way to make contact with Vega, so I'd tiptoe into my office before dawn cracked. I'd light white candles at each of the Four Cardinal Directions, as my Indian friends do in sacred ceremony, I'd pray for protection and guidance, then wait to see if anything would happen. In the beginning, my rational mind waged war a lot, telling me I needed sleep more than I needed this nonsense.

Then Vega would appear, bathed in Light – stern and calm and authoritative, and the teaching would begin. My doubts would fall away and I would listen and write, interjecting questions, anxious for answers.

The first series of messages were about the future of the planet and its inhabitants, and the message was clear. We on planet earth, are in a countdown to cataclysm, but we're being given extraordinary coaching in hope we won't fail the test this time, as it seems we have done, several times before in earth's history.

"The day of reckoning for this planet is not far off now," Vega said. "Your species wishes to make the leap of consciousness, but it wallows in self-deception and has allowed it's conscience to be lulled by pleasures. There are many who would choose otherwise, if they were aware of the dangers to themselves and to their children."

What Vega was saying was not what I wanted to hear. I'd recently gotten beyond a very sad divorce and was gravely in need of good news. The vision he provided was of hardship and tough choices. And I still didn't know if I could trust him.

I've always thought of my psychic gifts as being something like a short-wave radio set – psychics pick up more bands than most people do. Our radio sets aren't perfect, but they allow us a wider range of input than what's available to everybody else. I believe we simply utilize some portion of the 90% of the brain capacity that science says lies dormant in most people. So I was wary of Vega – just because I was "picking up" transmissions from some new waveband, didn't mean I was tuned in to the right station.

Many years before, I'd studied trance-mediumship with Ethel Meyers Johnson, a renowned medium who was Arthur Ford's chief disciple. Ethel had told me I had the "gift," but she'd warned me to be very careful about ascertaining who was coming through to me in any channeling session, as many dangerous, ill-informed or thoroughly malevolent entities from the astral plane attempt to subvert neophyte mediums.

"Just because someone's dead doesn't mean he's any smarter or better intentioned than when he was alive, dear," she'd cautioned, "and the disembodied are not necessarily reliable unless they come from a very high vibration." I'd shied away from my channeling gift for many years, both because of her admonitions and because of my practical nature. I couldn't let myself be lured into something so uncertain and unquantifiable. Nonetheless, I'd had some pretty astounding psychic experiences over the years – I'd studied with Medicine Men, Shamans and Spiritual Healers, so I knew enough to be wary of taking any wooden nickels from Vega, just because he was disembodied and capable of communication.

As the days wore on and the messages continued, I got bolder. I asked Vega where he'd come from. He said he was an emissary of the Forces of the Light and that he'd come from Vega, 26,000,000 light years away and our closest star neighbor in the cosmos.

I found his being an ET, not an angel, very disturbing. Like most people raised as Irish Catholics I had no trouble at all believing in the Angelic Realm. According to Time Magazine's survey, 69% of people believe in angels and/or have had contact with one. But ET's were something else again.

Some quick research revealed that Vega is the brightest star in the Summer Triangle and the fifth brightest star in the night sky. It has a diameter almost three times that of our Sun. Fourteen thousand years ago, Vega, not Polaris, was our Pole Star. I learned that life-bearing planets, rich in water could possibly exist around Vega. But even if that were true, I asked myself, how could communication from such a distant source take place?

Vega would leave and my rational mind would go into overdrive with unanswerable questions. Who was he, and why was he talking to me? I'd had plenty of proof over the years that communication with other dimensions was possible. I was Irish, and I'd been born with a caul over my face, which is the Irish harbinger of Second Sight. I'd seen many other lifeforms in the Universe over the years when working with Shamans, Healers and Tribal Medicine Men and Women, and I'd always been blessed with the ability to see angels. But communication with angels was one thing talking to an unknown Star Visitor was something else entirely. How could I be sure it wasn't my imagination tricking me? If not that, and if this communication was genuinely from some other dimension of reality, how could I be certain of the motives of the entity I was talking to? What was his agenda? Where had my trusted guides gone and why? I kept trying to contact them, but to no avail.

"Why exactly should I believe *anything* you tell me," I asked Vega one tired, skeptical morning.

"I am simply an intermediary for other Intelligences who wish to speak with you and through you," he answered calmly. "For eons, we Vegans have acted in concert with the Great Mother, EarthMother Gaia and other Celestial Deities, when they wish to speak with earthlings or transmit information through a human vehicle."

"But why would they want to talk to me?" I pressed. It seemed to me they were making a pretty serious mistake for Celestial Deities.

"You have been an oracle priestess in many incarnations, Alana," he replied. *Alana?* What did that name mean to me? He raised his hand in the gesture I now realized opened some doorway in my perception that allowed me to see things ordinarily hidden.

As his hand crossed my face, visions arose in me with nauseating clarity, of past lifetimes in service to many deities, over vast stretches of time. Weird energies swirled through me as I saw gods, goddesses, other entities who'd been worshipped as deities, some from such ancient cultures we no longer even have conscious memory of their existence. Each had left a specific imprint on my soul that was momentarily accessible to me. The vision left me reeling – and desperate to know more.

"You have the capacity to receive The Mother's transmissions and those of others," he said. "But certain work must be done on your physical/energetic body in this lifetime, in order for you to carry the vibrational frequency of these powerful disembodied Intelligences. I am the overseer of this work, but I must have your permission to begin." I had a sudden flash of myself as some cosmic engineering project, and didn't know whether to laugh or cry. But I was intrigued enough to say yes.

I gave Vega permission for the work to be done on my body, feeling as Magellan must have when he boarded the ship bound for Cathay.

CHAPTER 3

Reincarnation

It was obvious that in order to accept The Celestials' message, I'd have to accept the fact that I'd lived before. Considering my Irish Catholic roots, you may be wondering why I was able to do that, so there are a few things I'd best tell you about my life before the Celestials entered it.

I've always had some kind of "far memory." Even in childhood, events from other lives, in other historical time frames, would sometimes unfold for me without warning. When I was young, I didn't understand what was happening, so for many years I tried to convince myself it was just an overactive imagination at work. It wasn't until I was 12 that I ever found evidence that my memories were verifiable. I stayed overnight in a house I'd never visited before, only to awaken the next morning with the clear knowledge of the family who built it in

1829. At the local historical society and in the town cemetery I was able to verify all the names and information my dream vision had shown me.

Some of the past lives I accessed were extraordinary, some mundane, some fraught with terrible hardship. In some I was male, in some female, sometimes I wielded power, well or badly, sometimes I barely eeked out existence. I even found myself *between* lifetimes once, in a place of learning and respite. It was obviously not the Purgatory of my Catholic Sunday School Theology – instead, it was a place of understanding and clarity beyond what can be experienced in the body.

I didn't in the least understand my psychic gifts – in fact, I often tried to deny or evade them. It wasn't until I was long grown that I first had a chance to integrate this past life knowledge into the wider reality of my current life.

I come from a family in which the female line is undeniably gifted with clairvoyance, or, as the Irish call it, Second Sight. Different gifts manifested in different women – healing, psychic ability, telepathy, the ability to predict death, seemed to pop up randomly. You can't live around such gifts without being aware that there's more to life than what most people see. You also learn not to talk about it to the neighbors.

I grew up seeing plenty of evidence that the unseen Universe not only existed but often intersected with the ordinary world. As I got older I began to study the sacred scriptures of the world's great religions, an experience that was like manna from heaven. Exposure to the Bhagavad Gita, the Koran, the Torah, and other sacred scriptures gave me a chance to see how relentlessly we humans seek God by endless roads. And how, absurdly, each organized religion believes itself to be the one true path. It comforted me to learn that three quarters of the planet shared my perception of past life experience. Hindus, Tibetans, many Tribal People, all accepted the idea that our souls are immortal and that they evolve through many embodiments on their strange and circuitous route to wherever it is we're going.

Nonetheless, I spent a lot of years trying to impose rationality on what extra sensory gifts I had, and, to my endless detriment, too often ignored my psychic "knowing" in favor of what my rational mind could prove. But the one fact that was always clear to me was that either I'd lived often before, or I had the gift of retrieving from my DNA the experiences of others in my genetic lineage. I had such visceral memories of other time-slots, and *knew* so intimately how people thought and felt in other times, that I began writing it all down, then checking with historical societies and reference works to ascertain whether or not the remembered landscapes were valid or just my imagination. When I wrote facts with conviction born of my past life memory and research confirmed that they were true, I began to feel certain I'd lived many times before and for whatever inexplicable reason a great deal of what I'd experienced in these other lives remained available to my current consciousness.

So by the time The Celestials decided to put me through Cosmic Boot Camp, the one part of the experience that wasn't difficult for me to accept was the idea that I'd lived before.

CHAPTER 4

Work on My Body

During the entire first two years of the Celestials' transmissions, they worked constantly on my "physical vehicle," so I'd be able to channel the necessary frequencies for their message. The Vegan planetary intelligence was so far beyond our own, Vega explained, it allowed feats of physical and energetic engineering we can't yet conceive of, which is why their technologies were frequently utilized for a project like the one in progress. Vega's "project" had very real physical repercussions for me. I didn't know whether to be thrilled there was finally concrete proof of *something* going on, or be disturbed by the pains, aches and illnesses that were the fallout of their incessant tinkering with my body.

As the work progressed, I could psychically "see" those who did it, so I began to divide them into categories: The "engineers," appeared to affect structural changes with major physical impact. Their work made my bones hurt or creak or adjust radically, as if a cosmic chiropractor had me in his grip. The "doctors" went briskly about their soft tissue work without consulting me – afterwards, I usually found myself in respiratory distress, or with an accelerated heart rate or a severely sore throat that would disappear in a few hours. Later, it would be the Celestials themselves who, seemingly impatient with the others, would take charge of the work to expedite it. But during the first few months Vega was obviously calling the shots.

I had throat and breathing problems that he assured me were a result of the work being done on me. "The matter of your physical body must be dealt with," he said when I complained. "We have done work on many of your systems – physical, energetic, emotional and spiritual – in order for you to carry the frequencies in the way that you must, to do the task assigned to you. The respiratory ills are due to this work. Certain physical changes have taken place that will cause you to be vulnerable in your own world, for a time." He got that right. During that year, I picked up every respiratory germ in a ten mile radius.

At times I was told to follow a vegetarian diet, at other times, told not to. I was to drink more water, walk as exercise, and do Qi Gong and other Martial Arts to stay fit.

Sometimes Vega's explanation of what they were doing to my body brought along intriguing information as a bonus. One morning, as I coughed and struggled to speak through laryngitis, I was told, "This illness will now pass and your throat will be suitable for our work. The human form is an extraordinarily versatile vehicle. When the physical matrix was designed, the Celestials incorporated potentials not yet dreamed of by your race. As your soul knows, in the beginning, telepathic and matter-transformative capabilities were commonplace on this planet, but in those times there was no need for many of your other capacities, like courage or fortitude. As one gift wanes, another waxes. In the Golden Time to come, all gifts will be activated and all strands of DNA original to your unaltered species will again be implanted and activated."

It seemed a good cue to ask what they meant by "unaltered" and who it was who had altered us in the first place. But it would be a good long while before I got any answers. At least it was comforting to know a "Golden Time to come" was in the offing.

CHAPTER 5

Gaia

All through that first strange year, life bombarded me with so many challenges I was dodging flak at every turn. I was lamenting all this to Vega one morning, when he told me that Mother Gaia, the Intelligence that animated planet earth, would now speak to me directly. My petty complaints about housing and life didn't seem to be on his agenda.

I hadn't a clue how a planet could speak to a human, and said so irritably. Up to that moment, I'd thought of Gaia as a made-up anthropomorphic metaphor created to help us feel a sense of kinship for our home world. "How exactly will She speak to me?" I asked with plenty of attitude, and no reverence whatsoever. "What exactly does the voice of a whole planet sound like?"

As I said the words, a stomach churning shift took place in my vibrational field – an intense ripple on a molecular level that heightened my perceptions and radically altered the vista before my eyes. As if a curtain had been drawn away, I found myself staring into a cobalt blue Infinity, against which a magnificent figure could be seen. The form was vast and female. The giant orb of planet earth seemed inter-woven with her body, as if her energies and the planet's energies were inextricably intertwined. Energy lines crisscrossed the planet surface like an electrical grid... huge vortexes of energy pulsed and swirled, providing life force to the earth itself. I could see that her Beingness extended far beyond the perimeters of the planet, into the deep mysterious cosmos. *How* I could see all this, I can't explain. That I *could* see it was so mind-bending I didn't know what to do.

A voice rang in my head. It was mellifluous and kindly, but resonant as an ocean. It exuded energy that was decidedly female and overwhelmingly passionate. It was instantly apparent why the Native Americans call the Earth "Mother." This primordial archetypal intelligence radiated maternal power.

Awestruck as a child, I stood speechless. I was just a speck of dust in the cosmos compared to this immense Being, but I could hear Her and see Her, and that was more than enough. Weirdly, I felt as if I'd come home. She called me Alana Earthchild and my daughter Vraya; She said She remembered us, and there was much work to do in an urgent timeframe. She began to tell me the truth about Planet Earth. She said there were serious times to come.

The vision ended, I sat in stunned silence, trying to get my heart to stop pounding enough so I could breathe. Tears rolling down my face, I just kept saying thank you, thank you, *thank you*, Mother, in hopes that she'd understand how grateful I was for the astounding privilege of meeting Her.

But what seems plausible and real at such a moment of revelation at 5AM in the quiet darkness, seems very different after the moment fades. By 10AM, I'd decided it just couldn't have happened the way I thought. By 12, I was trying to put it all on paper. By 5 in the afternoon, I'd decided the whole thing was insane and ridiculous, so I didn't sit to channel at dusk, for fear of a return performance. But by 5AM, I was back in my office where I usually prayed, hoping with all my heart She would return.

And return, She did.

In the early days of Gaia's message there was sometimes interference in the transmission, a sort of cosmic static that interfered with the Voice. Each time this happened, the etheric "engineers" and Vega would appear again to tinker with my circuitry. The good news was that the sounds became clearer and stronger; the bad news was that Gaia's message was frightening. As the information became more and more detailed and complex, my elation at being Her messenger was tempered by the gravity of the message. I began to be seriously alarmed by it.

Gaia told me we were nearing the end of a cosmic cycle lasting 25,865 years. She explained that at the end of such great time cycles – and there had been countless ones for Earth – She must shrug herself back into alignment with the intergalactic electromagnetic grid. Each time She does this necessary action, She said, in order to keep the planet in orbit, great geophysical changes happen on earth. Sometimes the poles shift, sometimes they reverse themselves completely. (I later learned that scientists believe because of geological evidence that the poles have reversed on earth more than 160 times.) Before the last such shift, Vega, not Polaris, was our pole star, and always there are major cataclysms, such as the Great Flood chronicled in the Old Testament, or the Ice Age. The next such shrug is scheduled for the early part of the 21st century. She said this was inevitable.

"If it's inevitable," I asked, "why even bother to send this message? If we can't avoid disaster, what possible good is served by knowing of it?" She replied that the shrug was only one part of the picture and would not necessarily cause calamitous damage – that it was simply one part of the equation. Gaia said that terrible damage is being done to Her by greedy and conscienceless businesses and governments. She detailed the need for humanity to raise its consciousness to a new and far higher level of vibration in order to counter this disastrous pattern.

"Each time a great cycle nears an end," She said, "an opportunity opens for humanity to take a quantum leap forward as a species. The next leap for you will be the shift from third to fourth and fifth dimensional consciousness. In this planet's vast history of such pivotal moments, humanity has sometimes passed and more often failed, as the Ice Age attests, but this time, great cosmic aid is being offered to you to help you overcome the obstacles and expand your awareness toward cosmic consciousness. This help is coming to you from the level of deity, and from a variety of extraterrestrial sources far more highly developed than your species, whose collective progress is being hindered by the fact that your species is lagging behind them. You will not be permitted to destroy the planet itself, for it occupies an important place in the Cosmic Design, far beyond your comprehension."

She said we might, however, succeed in destroying ourselves.

She said if we did not make radical changes in ourselves and our treatment of the environment, the world as we know it would cease to exist.

CHAPTER 6

The Deer

Gaia's message really disturbed me. Feeling awestruck and privileged to be talking to Her, I also felt scared to death. Not just by the distressing news, but by the responsibility. It's one thing to be chosen as a messenger, quite another to figure out how to get anyone to believe the message. I couldn't conceive of a way to tell this story without being branded a nut case and my credibility as a rational person was key to my livelihood. Why wasn't this message given to someone with the power to change things? I asked repeatedly. No answer came.

My channeling sessions became sporadic. I began to feel angry and rebellious about what was happening to my body. I didn't want to be sick on top of being so hard-pressed by other problems. And, I didn't want any more responsibility or any more bad news. I told myself I was having major pangs of rationality about my channeling, but the truth was, I had a very hard time coping with the news I was receiving and what it seemed to demand of me.

During channeling, I never doubted for an instant what I was seeing and hearing – The Divine Intelligence that was Gaia overwhelmed me, thrilled me, buoyed my spirit, made me believe there really was a way to spread the word. But later, in the cold clear light of everyday hardships and uncertainty, question marks were everywhere. If this message was really divinely inspired why was everything in my life falling apart? If The Celestials really wanted me to be their messenger, why wasn't I being given help? What if this information were wrong? What if I went public with it and caused a panic? And what would happen to my credibility in the "real" world, if I told people I was talking daily to the disembodied energy of planet Earth? It sounded ridiculous even to me.

I felt spiritually bi-located – living two separate lives in two separate worlds and I didn't feel I had the strength for both. Some days, I'd drag myself out of bed at 4:15 AM, walk the dog in pitch-blackness, praying for guidance and feeling like a complete idiot. Then I'd settle in to channel, the Light would come and nothing in the world seemed more important than being the scribe for the Message. But then, dawn would break. Bills would need paying, work needed to be done and going back down the psychic rabbit hole seemed the last thing I would ever want to do.

I decided I needed a sign that would break the awful log jam of uncertainty in my mind. Driving all alone along Route 22 at dusk one night, feeling deeply troubled and frustrated by my inability to come to a satisfactory conclusion in the quiet privacy of my car, I cried out aloud to Gaia. I begged Her to send me an unmistakable sign that would prove to me it was truly *She* I was speaking to. Later, I realized the hubris of such a mad request – ask the Earth Mother for a sign and you're lucky if you don't get struck by lightning.

No sooner had the words left my mouth, than a huge buck leaped from the woods at the side of the road and smashed into my car door on the driver's side with such force it drove me off the highway. Stunned into that bizarre slow motion that overtakes you at the moment of life-threatening events, I clearly saw the deer's eyes just inches away from my own. I watched his spirit leave his body and I knew with absolute certainty that, in some bizarre way, he was my answer. Later, a State Trooper told me he'd never before seen a deer crash into the side of a car in just this way. Usually they get startled by headlights and are hit head on, he said. Broadsiding a car in this fashion was very rare. "You didn't hit the deer, lady," he said, with a quizzical look on his face, "that deer hit you."

Shaking with emotion as I stood looking down at the poor dead deer crumpled on the pavement at my feet, I felt horrified that my lack of faith had precipitated his death. Barely able to see through my tears, I got back into my car and drove to the home of a medicine woman friend, where I blurted out my story. She suggested we do sacred ceremony for the deer's spirit and that we use our friend Rosalyn Bruyere's system of trance mediumship to ascertain what was really going on with my channeling.

"I think the only way you can safely continue channeling," she said, thoughtfully, after hearing my story, "is if a Gatekeeper from the Celestial Plane, far above he Astral, will agree to be your protector on the Other Side."

We prepared a sacred space and, still heartsick about the deer, I prayed that a Celestial Gatekeeper would be sent to guard and guide me in my channeling efforts. Minutes passed with no response to my plea. Just as I was about to tell my friend this was a hopeless waste of time because I was still so unnerved I couldn't center my energy, a column of brilliant golden white Light sprang up around me like a forcefield that reached upward to infinity. Energy like molten electricity zinged through my body and I became aware of an immense archetypal male presence, which had arisen behind me. The intensity of love and goodness radiated by this Being exuded power like the sun. His energy field enfolded me so overwhelmingly, I was unable to move or speak.

We began to accelerate upward through the column of other-worldly Light at warp speed. I heard sounds – angelic laughter? ethereal music? the tinkling of what sounded like cosmic wind-bells, incredibly exquisite sounds – as I hurtled through the whirlwind.

I wondered if I might be dying.

We passed through dimension after dimension – etheric, astral, angelic planes raced by us – before we finally came to rest in a place of such resplendent Light, no earth words could convey it's splendor.

The upward rush halted and I saw standing before me an indescribable figure. Vast, radiant, regal beyond any Queen who ever lived, She was unmistakably the Great Mother Intelligence that emanates all female power in the Universe. Called Isis, Mary, Ishtaar, Inanna and a thousand other names in different lands and times – to me, in that moment, she was simply, unquestionably the Divine Mother.

She smiled. The radiant kindness of her gaze calmed me like balm. "You have been granted a Celestial Gatekeeper, Alana, so you can channel My Message in safety," She said, in a voice so mellifluous and powerful it seemed capable of bringing worlds into being. "A time of female empowerment is surging onto your planet and the Message needed by humanity will be transmitted through the female energy stream this time, just as last time it was transmitted through the male consciousness."

So began the relationship which I'll try to recount for you on the following pages. There are now over a thousand pages of handwritten transcript, so I'll do my best to explain the Message, as best I understand it. Wherever possible, I'll use the exact words I heard from The Celestials.

I've been told by Them that the great archetypal Intelligences of the Celestial Plane have been known by so many names in so many places, that it isn't important that they be addressed by specific names. They reveal themselves in different generations and locations, in differing forms, in order to make their words accessible to humans, so we can more comfortably be guided by their Divine teachings.

They've told me that the ancient names by which I call them may carry too much historical baggage for many readers. If this is so, They ask that you simply think of them as The Mothers or the Celestials, so their Message can be received into your heart without interfering with your current belief system. They say if you're meant to hear, you'll hear – if you're meant to understand, absolutely nothing can stand in the way of that understanding.

Their Message is about humanity's uphill climb toward enlightenment, about the past and future of Planet Earth, and how we can save it and ourselves. It's about the female paradigm that's beginning to flood the world – a consciousness that will allow us to access new ways to accomplish our goals. This is by no means a consciousness that excludes men, rather one that will be shared with all men of good will who choose to receive it and participate in the Great Work. It's been made clear to me over and over again in this channeling, that men and women are meant to be respectful partners in the work of saving our planet, humanity and all sentient lifeforms.

I urge you to filter all knowledge gained in the Message that follows, through your own inner knowing. Judge their truth by what they ask of you.

Whatever seems to resonate for you, keep and use for your own good and for the good of all.

Together, maybe we can change the future for the better. Such change is always done, not by governments or by vast institutions, but by individuals of like mind and conscience bonding together for the common good. The Mothers said to think of this kind of common cause as Groundswell.

PART II

Planetary Dangers to the Earth and to Us

CHAPTER 7

The Rape of the Planet and Our Food Supply

"So much of beauty has been given to your people, mortal, yet they have wreaked so much havoc," was the way I was greeted by a seemingly distressed Gaia, one early morning.

"The Earth suffers gravely in many places. Mountains are being leveled to extract coal. Whole ecosystems are destroyed without conscience. Water is becoming poisonous all over the planet. Children and adults are being made ill by pesticides and by the by-products of plastic in all they consume. Brain patterns are altered by television and electronic gadgetry.

"The water that feeds my children and that covers my body is being harmed – all must be given awareness of this danger. If the poison becomes too pervasive, I will be forced to remove the poisons by massive destruction. Many people will die in the cleansing. Much filth will be released to humanity's detriment. You must work to make people aware and conscious, as you work to help them survive."

"But what can any one person do to stem the tide?" I asked feeling pretty inadequate to the task of cleaning up the whole ecosystem of the planet.

"Humans destroy their own habitat at a rate that makes it impossible to replenish," Gaia said. "Greed is the conscienceless bias of humanity in this time. Those at the top pull the strings below, and most do not understand the magnitude of the destruction. You must tell them what's happening. Even if you feel like Cassandra, doomed to tell the truth and not to be believed, you must make this your crusade. Begin to speak and to raise the roof about the issue. Activists change the world."

I thought about Rosa Parks and Martin Luther King Jr. About Sojourner Truth and Mrs. Pankhurst and all the other crusaders who had stood against the established order. I knew it was always individuals, not bureaucracies, who make change happen, it was just pretty hard to imagine myself in such courageous company, and I said so. Gaia reminded me that I'm not alone in receiving this Message.

"There are countless men and women who toil to create, to save, to salvage, and to restore. This is a most volatile time for humanity – even We who see all future time lines are fascinated by the possibilities among you now, and by your ingenuity as a species. More than all this, it is the heart and soul of your species that causes so many of your people to choose goodness not greed, in the face of overwhelming odds."

Concern About our Food Supply

She said we must act quickly for the poisoning of our species is escalating dangerously and causing an enormous acceleration of fatal illnesses like cancers. She said this danger would escalate exponentially in the next decade if we did not halt the poisoning.

"The destruction of your food supply is a far worse danger than your species realizes," Gaia said. "Genetically altered foods (later called Frankenfoods, GMO's or GE's) have already taken hold in the world. Genetically engineered corn and other vegetables are commonly used in all packaged foods. The same is true of fruit to a lesser degree, but it is just as deadly." She said, "Seeds are being made sterile in order to makc seed companies richer. If seeds can't propagate, people will soon be unable to feed themselves unless they purchase new seed from those who control the market." She said the GMO'd seeds would contaminate not only people but other crops so that finding appropriate food for human consumption would become nearly impossible.

She said that insecticides would be genetically engineered into foods so that people would be harmed insidiously without knowing what was happening, and that terrible diseases would proliferate because of these seed alterations. At the time it seemed implausible, but now, 15 years later, pesticides are being engineered into large parts of our food supply as a matter of course.

"The soil is contaminated by nuclear and industrial waste. My rivers are dying; my fish and game are leaving the earth as whole species, at an unprecedented rate. The planetary food supply is becoming all but synthetic and not as nature intended it for the nourishment and healing of humanity.

"A chain of events is set in motion by this disastrous greed. Un-natural foods are created. They are eaten by animals and humans. They are also eaten by the animals you eat as food. The pigs and cows and chickens are altered and become disease-prone. Antibiotics must be administered constantly to hold this at bay. What you eat has less than 50% of the nutrients you believe it has.

"You and the animals are falling prey to new diseases that have no cure in nature because they have no cause in nature. Your physiological systems and those of the food chain were created to interact and replenish each other. All disease once had a cure in nature. All health could be sustained by what was grown on this planet. When man genetically re-engineers what is consumed, he cannot similarly re-engineer the consumer. Genetically engineered crops and altered animals do not provide correct energetic materials for the survival of your species.

"The balance of the ecologically correct insect-to-plant-to-animal ratio is out of harmony. Old species die off too fast for nature to create controls through replacement of species. The insect/mosquito problem you face (encephalitis bearing mosquitoes were in the news) was not bred by nature but by man, as a biological warfare experiment, but other plagues of diseases borne by mutant insect species will soon be upon you (Insects that carry nano-viruses and tracking devices now exist having been created by the military). Other species of insect life necessary to the cycle of growth and harvest on your planet will be injured or destroyed so they cannot pollinate." (Bee colonies are currently dying at an unprecedented and inexplicable rate.)

As if that wasn't depressing enough news, the next morning Gaia said, "I wish to speak today of the water on your planet. There is industrial waste being pumped into my rivers and oceans. Nuclear and industrial contaminants are buried in the soil and leaching into the water tables. My rivers are used as garbage dumps. My fish and sea creatures are dying in unprecedented numbers. My replenishing rain is contaminated with the detritus of atomic and nuclear explosions.

"The oceans are bombarded by noises that disturb the dolphins and injure my children of the deep. The dolphins have extraordinary knowledge to share with humanity and have been waiting eons for your species to become evolved enough to receive their message. Those in captivity have sacrificed their freedom to make the necessary connections with your species. The proliferation of noises disrupts their sonar and their sound-wave based communication systems in a disastrous way. Man contaminates first, then he cleans, and the accumulation of illegal substances that have been consigned to earth and water is changing the growth cycles of the planet, as well as of the other species you humans cannot sustain life without.

"Nefarious people are attempting to patent the molecular structures of my waters, and to control water sources. Insidious deals are being made by governments and giant corporations that will constrain the freedom of waterways and water access. Water will become scarce in your lifetime, and those who control it will have true power, as has been the case in days gone by."

That idea seemed preposterous in the 1990s, until an Indian activist friend, who worked with indigenous tribes in South America, gave me specific information that corroborated this bizarre fact. Huge conglomerates are actually patenting the molecular structure of waters in many places throughout the world, she said. Having gathered documentation while researching in South America she was planning to present her information to U.N. investigators, and was intent on embarking on a crusade to expose the truth. Shortly after our conversation she was killed by rebel forces in South America. It was reported as a terrorist act, but I've often wondered if she might have been silenced by the forces she sought to expose.

"You have seen my fairies," the Mother continued, "You know how many creatures work to sustain the environment. They, too, are gravely endangered." The summer before, Dakota and I had spent an amazing night on a mountain in North Carolina that was said to house a fairy grove. We'd waited several hours in a wild garden by the side of an immense lake, and been rewarded by seeing a group of strange balls of light of varying sizes (ping pong ball to baseball size), glowing with soft pastel colors – they surrounded us so closely we could actually feel their energies brush by us. They encircled us, as if assessing our intent, then nestled in the trees, and finally surrounded us again, before wafting off into the deep woods. It was a lovely magical experience and we'd been told by the owner of the property, a remarkable mystic named Rev. Marian Starnes, that the fairies and other earth elementals are responsible for all growth cycles in the vegetable and plant kingdom.

"Help must come from humanity," the Mother said. "Humans must stop the rape and pillage of my water and my earth. Humans must realize they cannot live on this planet if they destroy the eco-structure. Time is running out for many species on your planet. While over the eons many creatures have come and gone, the loss at this time is unprecedented. All was conceived in balance. A singular orchestration of balanced energies and life forces, each of which sustained its fellow life forces. It becomes imperative that your human species understand that each link in the chain has a reason to exist from the lowliest to the most complex and august.

"The decimation of untold species of plant and animal life creates a domino effect that ends at the top: humanity. The rainforest, the water supply, soil pollution, genetically altered foods, pesticides, poisons in the guise of medicines that cure one ill and create another, all these, too, are links in a chain of destruction. You must get the message out."

"But Mother, why would anyone listen to me?" I asked deeply alarmed by the urgency of Her speech. "And what power do individuals have against such huge odds?"

"You will speak My Truth," She answered unhesitatingly, "and it will be recognized. I have spoken in the past of individuality in your species. It is one of your strongest and most peculiar points of difference from most life in the galaxy. You are not a hive mentality; you are communal but individual. It is this individuality that drives you (humans) and that can save you now from extinction.

"It is never bureaucracies that cause change for the betterment of humankind. It is individual humans who rise to the demands of the moment and fight back, rallying their fellow humans to a cause greater than themselves. But, first they must be educated to the need. Thus do We intervene now for your survival.

"There is a long period of falling off, during which decimation of many kinds takes place and it appears that no harm has been done. Then a moment of truth is reached and the proliferation of decimations reaches critical mass. When that occurs, a domino effect is set into motion. It is as if the human species believes it can start an avalanche, change its mind and stay the avalanche from running its course. This is not the case.

"We of the Celestial Consciousness seek to intervene to stop the headlong rush to create the avalanche before it reaches critical mass."

"There is much to say. I wish to speak of my vibrations and that of the varied species on the planet. I operate as a pure intelligence, vast and powerful beyond the comprehension of mortals, as your intelligence is beyond the comprehension of the lowest animals. The embodiment I have chosen to show you in order to aid in the Divine Plan is that of this current planet Earth and all the earths that have occupied this place in the galaxy, for I have taken this planetary form on multiple occasions.

"The matrix of earth is holographically interwoven with the matrix of the original human species. As I have told you, this species has been interbred with dozens of others and DNA has been utilized in many ways to recreate species, so my vibration and the many vibrations on the planet have had to be recalibrated for each others' benefit over the millennia. This is not to say that I have changed, but merely that I have allowed evolutionary alterations in my pattern as was needed. Sometimes these alterations cause cataclysms, sometimes just evolution.

"You are at critical mass now for many manmade reasons. Tinkering with the atomic structure and the genetic code is extremely dangerous. Not merely in the ethereal and moral sense you are aware of, but in a vibrational integrity sense that is far beyond your comprehension except when you vibrate with Us at the Celestial rate. However, this knowledge cannot be brought back intact by you as yet.

"The danger of the tinkering is to the planetary home and to its critical spot in the galactic pattern. It will not be allowed that the current species destroy all. This is the reason so much help is pouring in to alter the future of your planet now. New species of babies are born daily. Babies of Light, as you call them, are here to harmonize (vibrations) and raise the bar.

"Others are here to stabilize and to anchor vibrations as they must continue for planetary stability. Certain humans act as pegs to anchor specific energies in place on the globe of Earth. Their density becomes essential to stability particularly at times of planetary geophysical crisis.

"Seven such (human pegs) must exist in physical form at all times to anchor the energies. Certain places on the planet perform the same function. When tribal people strive to preserve sacred lands like The Black Hills, they do so because they were instructed long ago that removal of the mineral wealth that resides there would alter the energetic grid of the planet that is needed for stability."

I later learned that Native Americans call the Black Hills in South Dakota, the "Heart of Everything that is." They believe the Earth Mother's body has organ systems just as we do, and that the Black Hills are the *heart* of the Earth. The Dineh (Hopi) Tribe believes its sacred Big Mountain is the earth's *liver,* and now that its coal is being depleted by mining processes that pollute and poison the surrounding land and water, the liver can no longer adequately cleanse the Earth Mother's body of toxic wastes. The Aborigines call the *Coral Reefs* the *Mother's blood purifier,* but now that our oceans are being so horribly polluted, the coral reefs are actually disintegrating. The Indigenous People of the Rain Forest believe that their forest forms the *lungs of the earth,* yet the Brazilian Government has approved the depletion of 50% of this oxygen-giving Sacred Site. The Gwich'In Nation calls the Arctic's National Wildlife Refuge, "*The place where life begins*", but oil drilling is killing off the lifeforms that begin there and setting off a domino effect of ecological losses unprecedented in earth history.

I asked what will happen if we can't set things right. The answer was pretty specific. "I have shown you that I wish to protect what I can of humanity." She referred to the fact that for the previous few months She'd been telling me in advance of impending earthquakes and explaining in detail how She worked to shift underground stresses in an effort to cause as little loss of life as possible.

"But the destruction behind the scenes," She continued, "the corruption, the govern-ment's biological experiments, the comtrail's, (chemicals spread by unmarked planes that leave a swath of unexplained respiratory and digestive illness in their wake), the poisons, the ecological rape that is practiced by those who know better – all these atrocities must be halted and *will* be halted. The Intergalactic Council will not permit this, and so the monitoring continues. If the balance tips too far, We will act and vast numbers will die.

"The underground movement of the tectonic plates in certain areas has been seriously impaired by nuclear testing, and by the extensive tunneling for the underground world that your government forces are constructing. They believe it will provide safety for themselves and their cohorts in a dire emergency. They are not correct in this assumption, and they undermine my physical structure with their extensive tunneling. I am disinclined to let humans and other hybrids suffer, but I must bring attention to the horrific acts that are endangering all alive here."

She told me to provide a map of the United States and to get a magic marker. When I did so, She had me draw a series of new outlines on the old map...an outline showing what the face of America will be, if the worst case scenario is enacted and major geophysical cataclysms become Her only means of protecting the integrity of the planet.

As my pen moved over the edges of the country, my heart sank. Most of the Eastern Seaboard disappeared, as did Southern California, Oregon and Washington. The great lakes formed a jagged, massive inland sea. A widened Mississippi completely divided the country, becoming a vast water channel that stretched from Canada to the Gulf of Mexico. The great cities of our current reality were laid waste.

I asked for clarification about why we find ourselves in this disastrous predicament: "Your world is in a time of great crisis," she said, "The earth suffers gravely and strives to keep the balance, even as mankind alters it daily, as if rushing to its own demise. Humankind has accepted as valid a non-human paradigm, in which intellect has outstripped heart, as the guiding force on the planet.

"The technological strides being made now are appropriate only if they are balanced by humanity's best strength, which is its heart chakra, its capacity for heroic compassion, and its desire to love and be loved.

"As greed has supplanted need, much of humankind has spent its efforts to *have* more, leaving those who have nothing to suffer. This is a perversion of the human strength given to your kind by Us eons ago, as an experiment. To *have* is one thing, to *be* is far greater. To become all that your biological and spiritual history allows is the goal of the upward spiral toward reabsorption to the God consciousness. We deities watch and wait. We have seen you fail and triumph. We have intervened at times to keep your planet intact and to keep the species viable in the face of new dangers."

I didn't like the sound of new dangers; we had plenty of old ones to cope with, so I asked Her to elaborate.

"There are new dangers coming soon. Virus that cannot be cured by antibiotics. Bacteria that will rampage throughout your world, if the imbalances are not set right. War, Famine, Pestilence, Death, the Four Horseman of the Apocalypse, are not merely poetic representations, they are truths that will ravage your world, unless you rededicate yourselves to each other, to truth, to compassion and to Gaia, to the Great Mother, and to the other Celestials who choose to recognize your species and help it evolve to its fullest capacity.

"These tests are arduous. They were devised to be. We are aware of your struggle and your suffering. We help in ways you cannot conceive, but we also expect much from you in return.

"Humankind grows lazy when it is given much of pleasure and abundance. Instead of sharing, it amasses more and more. Instead of looking to its suffering neighbors, it buys a bigger house. This is not the way to expand your souls, to grow in stature, into your true light and depth and breadth.

"Give and give now! Help and help now! Seek out the needy. Resonate at a level that raises the vibration of all humankind. Some are doing it. Emulate the best, the clearest, the kindest. Speak only the truth.

"The measure of each soul is weighed at death. In this time in which you live, the measure will be taken sooner, for much depends on raising the vibration of the entire planet swiftly.

"One human can touch all lives. It is the very nature of your being that all change comes by groundswell, not from the top, but from the individual who will not permit himself/herself to be less than what we expected when We created you.

"It is not yet too late. The time grows short, but it is *not* too late."

I told Her many of the problems She'd catalogued were already becoming known, yet people continue these destructive practices, that I didn't see what I could do to change the destruction without having some new kind of information to present that would galvanize humanity into action.

She said She would tell me the true history of the world.

CHAPTER 8

True History of Planet Earth

"You have asked before of your planet's history and been put off by Us," said the Great Mother, as She began Her story. "It is not an easy or linear question to answer. So many potent forces have converged on your planet, so many gods and so many seekers after their own agendas.

"Your species is an odd one – resilient, unpredictable, valiant and flawed. Yet because of your individuality and your hearts, which are both capricious and brave, you have drawn the attention of many.

"Colonizers have been here since time began. Hybridizers too numerous to name have entered your gene stream. The ones like you, who have psychic powers, are hybrids from other star systems or the angelic realm, although your matrix is human in the heart field, and, of course, your system has been honed and worked on in this embodiment, so it no longer resembles the human framework for energy." I wasn't sure that was exactly comforting, but it did at least sound like I was not alone.

"These mysteries have, in part, been made known to you because of your service in priestesshood in many incarnations. You have peered into the mysteries and been shown much. Your friend John Upledger worries about your desire to know beyond the veil, but you are merely striving to remember what had already been known.

"Your world is changing rapidly now," she continued. "Cosmic radiation and many off-world efforts combine to raise your vibrations as an entire global population and they are working for many as consciousness awakens and moves forward. There is much of wonder in the future of this world, but difficult terrain to traverse in order to get to the future. The Dark Force does not wish to be bested or laid low. Materialism lures many and lulls conscience. Businesses thrive that exploit and pillage. 'Human' nature admires the winner, even if the loser in the equation was in the right.

"The mistakes of the past, if they are repeated now, will bring your species to annihilation in a very short timeframe. Thus, vast amounts of Celestial Light are being poured onto your planet as We again intervene in your behalf. Your passage through the photon belt and the opening of a Stargate in January (of 2001) brings an influx of Light so vast it makes possible the casting off of the dark mantle that has enslaved you through millennia.

"The photon belt precipitates this acceleration on a molecular level. All movement from the tiniest atomic particle to the ponderous movement of your earth bodies, is being accelerated so that the frequency can be raised."

She said we would soon experience a sense of accelerating time in which we would feel propelled forward as if minutes, hours, days were growing shorter and shorter and were no longer adequate for accomplishing what we must on a daily basis.

"Your planet, of which I am The Great Intelligence, is lagging behind its sister and brother planets in this solar system," Gaia added. "The other Intelligences grow impatient to move forward interdimensionally and I myself grow restless for change. The difference is that I have grown fond of you mortals and hybrids who populate My World, and I do not wish to sacrifice any more than is necessary to the cause of moving forward intergalactically.

"Nonetheless, the time has come to shrug myself into the alignment necessary for stability. 25,000 years is long in earth time terms, but not so long in my terms."

The Mother paused, then spoke again. "I like the enterprising nature of humans and the capricious nature of the heart that at times surprises even me. But much of darkness has been permitted here and much of darkness rules. While the Plan unfolds and Creator observes possibilities as each race, planet, star system evolves and alters in an infinite web of possibilities and probabilities, the truth remains that your kind will not be permitted to destroy yourselves completely, or the planet, despite your pervasive greed and shortsightedness. So steps will be taken.

"The Creator's Plan is The Great Mystery, even to the Intelligences you call Gods – We, too, must watch and adjust in the great dance of Creation, for creation continues, every second of every hour, as you count such things.

"Celestial hands reach out to you now to help you rise as a species. But to do so, you must be told what has been kept hidden of your true past, so that you do not make the same mistakes and have to begin the climb once more from beneath the ashes of a fallen world."

What follows here is a shortened version of the very lengthy story I was shown and told by two of the Mothers:

"In the beginning was Creator, Who chose to experience Him/Herself through the emanation of other and varied lifeforms. The journey into matter for your kind was a long and arduous one. Godlings and angels were created before you, and were granted the same free-will that would later become your bane, as well as theirs. The war in Heaven in which the dark angels and other lifeforms you know not of, fell from grace, took place during these timeless eons, just on the edge of humanity's creation. Those events are now so long ago that only stories buried deep in the subconscious of humanity, in the legends of ancient tribes, and in age-old scriptural writings, hold clues to their existence.

"In the earliest times, those you now call Gods found this planet lovely and pleasurable. Many came here from another dimension and another planetary consciousness to enjoy the beauty and the sweetness of this world.

"I agreed to be the Guardian Intelligence that keeps the planet's integrity and for a time this was truly a place that was paradise."

I wondered if even Gods and Goddesses get trapped into responsibilities that are not easy to fulfill.

"But others envied us, and even among our own there was dissention and war," she continued. "Over eons Intergalactic forces came and went, leaving civilizations or leaving disastrous ruin in their wake. It was determined by the Wise Ones, who are beyond all knowing, that a Council would exist to use the earth's beauty as a laboratory for experimentation, with humanity itself being another experiment. You must know that many such experimental embodiments of portions of the God-intelligence exist in the Cosmos. It is a way for The Vast Intelligence to learn and grow within its all-knowingness.

"I realize that does not make it comprehensible for you, for it is a Mystery that cannot be fathomed by human intelligence. So much of what you've heard is true of wars and illusions foisted on you by others' agendas. Also true that humanity exceeded our expectations, both for good and evil, because of the inscrutable human heart and its abilities to love, to sacrifice, to be loyal and brave and enduring." The Great Mother said our heart is unique in the Universe. It is stalwart and capable of extraordinary feats because it *loves*, and is capable of remarkable feats of selflessness because of that, but it is also unpredictable. That higher planets populated by greater intelligences, lack this curiously unique and unpredictable heart capability that sets humans apart from other lifeforms.

"But the converse is also true; humanity can be cruel and perverse and dark – torturing, murdering and raping without conscience. We were appalled and fascinated and The Council decided to let the game play out within the Great Hologram of God.

"In ancient times, people knew of the game, just as they knew Us for We walked among them and intermarried if we chose. Our progeny still walk the planet in many guises.

"Unfortunately for the truth, many civilizations were highly developed enough to destroy themselves completely, so completely that the records of their very existence have been lost. Some records remain, of course, in crystals and in glyphs, some will be found in the Sphinx's Hall of Records. When the Church destroyed Alexandria and its priceless library, all became hidden, except to adepts who could read the Akashic, and there are hidden monasteries in Asia that preserve the texts of Lemuria and Atlantis. Of Adman little remains, and of Sieve, no trace can be found in this dimension." I had never heard these early civilizations named and to this day have found no record of a place called Sieve. (I'm not certain of the spelling as I only heard the word spoken.)

"What is known by very few is that not only angels fell from grace, but gods as well – godlings who had been emanated by Creator.

"As recounted in the Book of Genesis, some of these godlings still walked the earth, long after it was populated with humans and other lifeforms. In fact, their attempts to experience three-dimensional life led to self-gratification with vast repercussions for all species on your planet. At first they mated with animal life forms, pushing their vast minds into convoluted creations, part animal, part godling. After humans, too, had been conceived by Creator, they mated with them as well, and carelessly caused creatures to come into being that were grotesque and sometimes soulless. Fauns and satyrs, centaurs, mermen and mermaids, minotaurs, gorgons and other hybrids were created that now exist only in fantastic fables. There were also giants and cyclopses created, as well as certain tree forms in which spirits were entrapped in trees. The race memory of these times is reflected still in children's tales that tell of enchanted forests.

"This involution into matter from formless energy was a lengthy process – about four and a half billion years as you count time. Until the final entrapment in material substance was complete, many of the creations just recounted were closer to thought-forms than to material reality. Your world has remembered them as the myths that populate the oldest societies on earth. Africa, Asia, the Middle East, the Americas, the Pacific islands, all these lands have similar sacred stories that spring from the vestiges of this true memory that now seems implausible.

"When the great God Beings and the great Angels fell from Grace during this pre- and slightly post-human evolutionary time, your destiny as human beings who struggle with good and evil – spirit and matter – was set in motion, even before you had fully evolved as specific physical entities.

"It was about 15 million years ago when the godlings incarnated on planet earth in vast numbers, seeking the knowledge of what such a foray into matter might offer them experientially. They populated a vast landmass in what is now the Pacific Ocean. Sometimes called Mu or Lemuria by those who know of its existence, it was a dream-like Paradise, in which the godlings existed in a partly corporeal, partly etheric form. They communicated telepathically and experimented with pleasures in every conceivable way, as *experience* itself was their only goal. This period of primarily incorporeal involution lasted for millions of your years, during which time other Creations were brought into being in other places and dimensions. The Universe teems with life on billions of star systems that your science now barely begins to discern.

"The godlings could manipulate matter and they understood the energetic forces of nature in ways that made building on a giant scale quite ordinary. The Megaliths your scientists puzzle about worldwide, were in great measure built by these godlings, who had chosen gigantic size for their corporeal existence. Archaeological theory has no explanation for structures like the Great Pyramid of Giza and The Easter Island Statues, so it has hypothesized all manner of possibilities for how these stones were lifted into place, but as science has incorrectly dated these giant structures, the hypotheses are always incorrect. There have been many times on earth when power of this magnitude was commonplace, and many races of superior beings whose physical stature dwarfs your own.

"The unexpected evolutionary leaps in consciousness, the so-called 'missing links' in evolution, are attributable to interventions of various sorts by intelligences and powers far beyond yours. Is it really likely that only the passage of time – a mere

35,000 years between Cro-Magnan Man and the height of Egyptian civilization – could explain how such extraordinary progress was made? Time alone did not suffice. Intervention was the key.

"Countless times in the history of humankind, such deliberate interventions have been staged, both by Celestial entities and by extraterrestrial and extra-dimensional beings, so that your planetary consciousness can take a mega-step forward. Scientists have not found the 'missing link' between apes and man, because an intervention took place that side-stepped millennia of biological developmental time. Often, animal genetics were tampered with by species highly evolved enough to hold the genetic key. New codes were inculcated so that new possibilities could be experienced. And of course, once left to their own devices, many of these new lifeforms cross-mated and reproduced new strains of their own.

"The godlings and even the humans who eventually inhabited Mu, were not as dense in matter as the beings of later civilizations, so it is only the much later creations of totally material substance, like the Obelisks and Standing Stones, that remain for you to track.

"The godlings returned often, during the early millions of years of earth's infancy and childhood.

Each time they experimented, creating new thought-forms or material substances, so new species were born. They created some humanoid but soulless creatures, to be slaves and laborers, as well. When the godlings withdrew, they left these primitive beings behind to evolve on their own. Their progeny still exists on earth.

"Major cataclysms sometimes followed the godlings' experiments, as nature rebelled against their often indiscriminate use of the energies. Sometimes, they left of their own accord. Visitors from many star systems intervened and hybridized your planet. Some reigned for millennia, others merely left their seed and moved on.

"You are now in the 5th World. Four ancient civilizations as highly developed or a more highly developed than your own, have come and gone. Most have been so entirely obliterated, by their own mishandling of life or by nature's cataclysms that resulted from necessary realignments, that you don't even remember their names.

"Every ancient culture worldwide has multiple-creation scenarios in their religions or mythos because of these multiple world epochs. Most tell of continuing efforts to create humanoid creatures capable of existence in material substance, who still retain an awareness of Creator. The Maya, Aztec, Toltecs of Central America speak of these four "world ages," that have passed, the Navajo and Pueblo and Hopi in the Southwest remember these lost worlds as well. The Kabbalistic Jews have knowledge of the same four creations, as do the Hindus, and Tibetans. (I later learned from Guruji, who was head of the Jain Monks, that the Jains have 15,000 years of written history, and from Rinpoche H.H. Menri Trizin 33rd, Lungtok Tenpai Nyima, High Lama of the Bon Po Tibetans, that the Bon have 17,000 years of written history.)

"The Continent of Mu accounted for more than one World Age. The first was primarily ethereal, not material, a time of thought forms and mental existence rather than physical. The second commenced about 12 million years ago, when the Godlings began their serious experiments with corporeal existence. It was then that their incarnating took so many bizarre physical forms, as half-human, half-animal or even half-plant bodies were experimented with.

The Root Races

"When the Great War in heaven began for the power over earth's destiny, the people of earth were unaware of the role they played. The daughters of man had mated with those you call Gods – Gods walked the earth carelessly, embodying themselves in human form to partake of the pleasures of the flesh. There was less of struggle and strife than you would imagine. Earth had been used for colonization and rest by many, not only for her beauty, but also for her strategic positioning.

"As above, so below. When the battle began, the energies filtered down to the earth plane and began to inflame the peoples to discontent and revolution. There is a warrior element in your nature that had not yet surfaced, but as the energies changed to suit the needs of the Gods, so did the energies change in mankind. The Gods of war were happy with what they'd wrought. Those who loved the beauty of this planet and its inhabitants were horrified by the destruction and chose to continue to communicate with those mortals who could hear and see. Thus do We work through many to stabilize and to lead you out of darkness.

"The years of this particular phase of development was also the time when Lucifer and his rebellious army of angels, suffered the sin of pride and attempted a takeover of power from Creator. When Creator sent Archangel Michael to quell their rebellion, Michael and his vast army of loyal angels cast the rebels into the lower realms of both Hell and Earth. These godlings and angels – for both had fallen from grace – brought intense need for sensual gratification to earth with them, when they came.

"Many loyal angels attempted to help their fallen comrades retain cognizance of their Oneness with Creator, hoping to redeem them. But it soon became clear that the immersion into matter quickly contaminated the fallen to such a degree that they were all but unreachable.

"At this point, some enlightened godlings and angels chose to incarnate to help their wayward brethren. Thus, a second Root Race was born. They called themselves the Children of The One.

"A second body type emerged. It was designed to be better able to handle attunement to Creator, as well as life in the world of matter. Their bodies were far more powerful than yours, their energy centers or chakras were powerful electromagnetic forcefields that respired energy of both positive and negative polarities, in an endless loop of regeneration. Seven chakras (energetic wheels of light) reflected the seven colors of light that comprise your sun spectrum – red, orange, yellow, green, blue, indigo and violet – corresponding to root, naval, solar plexus, heart, throat, third eye and crown chakras. But these were merely the chakras of the physical system, while many more entry/exit points were respiring energy far above, below and beyond the physical.

"This time period was the one of godlings, monsters and human hybrids. As the loyal godlings became further bogged down in matter, it became harder and harder for them to shift in and out of Creator Consciousness, so they evolved a system of dream states, where the body was laid to rest and the spirit journeyed back to the Source for replenishment. Vast temples were constructed to protect and align the sleeping godlings with their powers, while their spirits traveled home. The temples were aligned to intergalactic energy fields to augment the godlings' powers with Celestial energies, particularly those of the Sun."

I had once had the chance to lie in the great sarcophagus in the Pyramid of Giza and had had a vision of initiates being interred there for a time as their spirits wandered the land in search of answers to the questions Initiation demanded, so what the Mother was saying struck a chord with me.

"The Children of Darkness envied the healing power and enlightenment of the Children of The One. As the Children of The One attempted to recalibrate earth's physical lifeforms to a less contaminted energy form, eliminating lower animal body constructions and using music, light and sound frequencies to raise their vibrations, the Children of Darkness fought hard to maintain their material world and all its sensual pleasures. They had been consigned to earth and considered it, and all its gratifications, theirs.

"War broke out. Discordance among godlings is an immense and powerfully disruptive force. The continent of Mu began to disintegrate, as the warring factions unleashed forces of the atomic energy of matter and manipulated the gravitational fields that anchored their thoughtforms to the planet. Gaia, the Earth Intelligence, rebelled and retaliated. Mu was shattered into pieces that for the most part, now lie at the bottom of the Pacific Ocean. All that remains of that exquisite garden Paradise are the scattered islands of the South Seas with their megalithic reminders of a time when gods walked the earth and erred as grievously as mortals.

"Many of the Children of The One fled Mu before the final inundation. Some went to what was destined to become North America, and in Arizona and New Mexico became the cliff dwellers and Indian tribes of the Southwest. Some went to Peru and Central America, Mexico and Guatemala, creating centers of early enlightenment. (Other colonizations took place around the Pacific Rim).

"Unfortunately, the battles had taken a toll. Both the Children of the One and The Children of Darkness were by then, deeply immersed in matter and its consequences. Each was equally determined to force its will upon the other.

"A Third World experiment was about to begin within the heart/mind of Creator. It would be called Atlantis and it is of Atlantis and its follies that your species needs to be most cognizant.

"Atlantis was the turning point into humanoid life as you know it. About 200,000 B.C. a new wave of incarnation emerged on a continent in the Atlantic. Mu's power was all but ended, although vestiges of its knowledge still existed. A new Root Race, which consisted of humans unmixed with animal or plant forms, would now succeed the previous one. Bodies were often hermaphroditic, encompassing both sexes, as had been the case with a large percentage of the population of Mu. Bodies were not static in their parts as they are today. They were shapeshifting, malleable forms that could call upon any sexuality desired at will. You think of hermaphrodites as mistakes that nature has visited on some unfortunate beings, but in those times to possess all sexual potential was ordinary and pleasurable. They could choose to accentuate either polarity for their own pleasure or for procreation. Souls were called in from the mind of Creator to inhibit the bodies of new children so conceived.

"This was a time of feminine rule, as conception could take place within the single being, and the predominant characteristic of those who ruled was female, as a reflection of Creator.

"The first true Garden of Eden was not (only?) in the Middle East but in Atlantis, where Creator chose to take a hand in the development of His/Her creations in a new way. Creator Him/Herself manifested a portion of Self, which we shall call the Logos of God, and this Logos actually incarnated in a form you can barely conceive of, to interact with humankind in a way quite different from before. "The Word," as the Bible says "became flesh and dwelt amongst you." This was done that you might learn from the Logos, and that the Divine Logos might *experience* through a new relationship with you.

"The Logos individuated male and female at this point in time, into separate bodies that could be complementary to each other. Oneness with each other and with Creator was to be attained through the coming together of these complementary beings. Later, as karma accumulated, the mandate changed somewhat and I will discuss this at another time, but in the beginning this was the Plan.

"Over the Millennia since then, there have been further incarnations of the Logos into male/female partnerships – you think of these as myths or religious truths, depending on your belief system. Amilius and Lilith, Adam and Eve, Hermes and Maat, Osirus and Isis, Jesus and Mary, are all human renderings – some accurate, some fallible – of such manifestations of the Logos, which was Itself, a manifestation of the One Creator. Thus the concept of Father/Son/Holy Ghost can be considered correct, only if the Holy Ghost is recognized as the Divine Feminine emanation."

Atlantis

Earth's true history was so vastly different from the one we'd learned of in the history books that now I was desperate to find out everything I could about it. References to Atlantis had come up on many occasions and the Mothers had said that a great number of Atlanteans had reincarnated in this current time. I asked for more specifics on the continent that so many thought merely a myth, and an explanation of its importance to us in our current planetary dilemma, which the Mother had earlier alluded to.

"Atlantis achieved a very high degree of civilization," the Mother replied. "In fact, much was as it is today on your planet. There was sophisticated technology that was run by lasers, powered by crystals of great magnitude. The knowledge of telepathy and the power of thought forms was still strong, and electromagnetism was an everyday concept taught to children by their tutors. The solar system and intergalactic grid were better understood than now and inter-dimensional travel was commonplace.

"Unfortunately, ethics and morality did not keep pace with this technology. Greed was pervasive and medical breakthroughs made it possible for humans and other hybrids to be cloned and duplicated in laboratories. The decision was made to use these clones as slaves and workers. As you know, clones may be perfect physical replicas, but they possess no divine spark, no soul that emanates from the Celestial Godhead as you perceive it, and therefore they were not only considered to be exploitable, they were *created* to be exploitable.

"Tragedies ensued over a period of many thousands of years because of the decaying morality of the Atlantean culture. Many tragedies born of the Atlanteans' short-sightedness have continued on this planet as a result, and many of those currently perceived to be human, are actually the progeny of the soulless ones, and do not come from the human lineage, except on a biological level.

"As we have told you, many Atlanteans have reincarnated in this current era to try once more to redress their follies. The world bears witness to their continued foolishness and there is no surety that they will do any better this time than the last time. The same errors of judgment appear to be happening once again, and they will be dealt with in the same way, if need be.

"The continent of Atlantis was destroyed by three separate cataclysms over a period of many thousands of years. Like the children of Mu before them, the highly psychicly skilled Atlanteans sent waves of priests, scholars and some royalty to places of safety before the final inundation. The British Isles, the Americas and Egypt all became sanctuaries to which initiates fled, taking with them their considerable knowledge of the history of the World, of your species' connection to the godlings and Creator, and of your connection to the other beings who inhabited the galaxy. They took, too, their skills in medicine, surgery, mathematics, building and architecture, astronomy, metalurgy and religion.

"The final earthquake/tidal wave that destroyed Atlantis was precipitated by a miscalibration of the massive crystal that powered much of the Atlantean capitol. This miscalibration disrupted the stability of the electromagnetic grid to such a degree that a quake of such vast magnitude ensued that the continent itself imploded and was plunged to the bottom of the Atlantic. The disruption of navigational equipment that occurs to this day in the Bermuda Triangle is due to the immensely potent frequencies of the doomed crystal that lies in the ruins of the Poseidian Temple deep beneath the waters of the Atlantic.

"This civilization – in which technology and greed grew exponentially neck and neck – was so completely obliterated, it was considered by later generations to be no more than a myth, despite the fact that Plato and other ancient writers recalled its existence with great specificity."

"Were there similar interventions in Egypt?" I asked, "and in Sumeria?"

I knew the Sumarian Tablets and Cylinder Scrolls and Seals from 5000 B.C. are reputedly the oldest written texts about earth's history that still exist in the west – at least the oldest that survived the burning of the Alexandrian Library. I now know there are older written records in the East – Tibet and India – but the Sumarian ones were a place to start.

"The Annunaki and Nephilim were colonizer-Gods, and Sumer was a place in which they seeded the new concept," was the reply to my question. I vaguely remembered the Nefilim from the Bible, but not exactly who they were.

"What new concept?" I asked.

"To allow a race to be enslaved that was somewhat conscious, but not in control. Programs were put in place to keep the Great Mystery Knowledge secret. Conversation with the Gods was limited, although more commonplace than in these later times.

"A veil of Forgetfulness and Unknowing-ness was strung around your planet. The net of Light Points you and others have seen (clairvoyantly) around Earth is the beginning of the breaking through of these veils of negativity. Many work with you. Many have been sent in and many have reincarnated to help you and those like you to succeed. Perhaps you now see that while the coming chaos and upheaval seems cruel, it will allow the Light to seep through the cracks and a new beginning to be made."

"But why did Creator or Universe or *whoever* allows, let this happen in the first place?" I asked, thrilled by my history lesson, but still confused about the motivation of Creator.

"It was part of The Plan," Gaia responded. "Your unfoldment as a species continues. Not merely here in this time/space, but on many worlds does this unfoldment maintain." Was the Plan, then, to create many species in many worlds, and experience life through all, then see which ones returned to their Source and how they got there? It all sounded like some bizarre cosmic game the Gods engaged in.

"If Atlantis was the Third Root Race," I asked, "who came next?"

"The Fourth World and the Fourth Root Race began with Adam and Eve," She said, "although Adam and Eve were not merely one coupling (evidently such couplings happened in many places). Many ancient lands had existed and perished by then, had come and gone and had generated migrations, so that life was already spreading into the Americas, China, Persia, Egypt and Europe in an almost simultaneous surge.

"The Fourth World is the place where your Biblical History of the World begins. Yahweh Elohiym, another manifestation of Creator, conceived a new plan for life on earth. He/She seeded life very specifically into five places as five separate races – the ones you are now familiar with – emerged into being, yet still resided within the Oneness that is God. (Presumably these new races spread out and intermarried with those already in existence? I should have asked for clarification.) The Biblical stories with which you are familiar take over at this point although, of course, they have been altered, mistranslated and misunderstood, as they've been passed on through countless generations and varied agendas.

"The beginning of the 21st century is the moment when the New Root Race, the 5th one to populate your earth, will truly begin to take hold. The Fifth Root Race is still emerging. It will bring with it an altered conscienciousness and enhanced spiritual and temporal abilities." She said that this newest race had the best potential so far to choose the high road.

"You are already in the 5th World and the 5th Root Race is already incarnating. The ones who can communicate beyond the boundaries of current time/space and the new children with unusual powers are part of this race, but many, many exist already on your planet. You, too, are among them as your ability to communicate interdimensionally attests."

I asked if Edgar Cayce's famous readings were really taken from the Akashic. The answer was intriguing. "Cayce was able to read the Akashic easily and well, but like all true mystics he fell heir to his own interpretation of much of what he saw there. His records are remarkably filled with Truth, but there were times when he incorrectly judged the scenes that unfolded before him and times when others have since taken his work and extrapolated from it, filling in certain blanks in their own ways. Much like the Bible, Cayce's vision has been somewhat rewritten over time.

"The Cayce material you have questioned is for the most part accurate in his history that was read from the Akashic. It is correct regarding the emanations of life from Creator and is correct in the overview of the past civilizations that have been on this planet. It is however incomplete in that he did not follow the development and decline of *all* civilizations that have populated earth. We will tell you of others. The Tibetan scrolls hidden for millennia contain the entire record – as much as can be written in a linear way. The Atlantean scrolls and tablets hidden in Egypt and the Yucatan supply much of the record (as much as can be written in a linear way). The Indian Vedas contain further fragments of what has existed. The Alexandrian library before its devastation was a similar depository of ancient knowledge and wisdom."

I asked how the otherworldly visitors and influences came to us.

"There have been many stargates on the planet you inhabit. Places where a powerful enough portal exists for vast numbers to come through. You experienced a large portal at a house you inhabited a short time ago. You had awareness of the traffic in otherworld entities that could come through such a rift in time/space. It was of course, not a rift in the sense of a wound of some kind, but rather a remarkable entry point, well understood by the native people who guarded it in other times."

I had once lived in a house that was on the National Registry of Haunted Houses. I didn't know this at the time I rented it, or that other-worldly entities would be living there, too. I probably should have been tipped off by the fact that the rent was quite low for a generally high priced neighborhood. An Indian Pipe Carrier, a Hawaiian Kahuna, an exorcist priest, a Cardinal's emissary, a Chinese Feng Shui Master and a number of major mystics (to say nothing of neighbors and friends) had all visited and experienced the strange phenomena of the house.

"Creation took place on many worlds beyond your own," the Great Mother went on. "It continues to take place there and visitors have been frequent. The fallen angels were not the only visitors to this planet whose own agendas changed the face of your history. Angels are intrinsically a separate species from man. They can of course appear to be godlings for their powers are vast, but they are not alone in having power in The Universe. Wars have been fought for control (of earth), and it would be difficult for you to separate out the many species who have colonized and populated the world ages of your race and the others on the planet.

"The evolution of life on earth took millions of years and several major interventions to achieve. Those whom you now refer to (collectively) as godlings have been angels, space visitors, interdimensional visitors, and Gods/Goddesses who were emanations of Creator's Divine Aspects and Choices."

It seemed what She was saying was that many histories of Earth were being played out simultaneously. It was little wonder that no lineal history could ever truly do it justice.

"The Solar Logos is a manifestation of Creator in which The Divine took flesh and experienced all of life and Earth in the human way. Needless to say, only the assumed flesh was capable of death, not the Essence of the Solar Logos. The Solar Logos was a Creation to help those *in* creation to maintain their direct connection to Creator, just as it was meant to help Creator experience that which He/She has created for a deepening of the bond of understanding."

Having attempted to put this all down on paper, I asked if I had left anything out.

"As to the history received as you wrote: there is so much more, so many millions of years, so many eons of side roads, of colonizations, of experimentation, of hybridization, of struggle and death and rebirth – it is impossible for a mortal to chronicle or understand all at this juncture of primitive thinking. A new wider range of understanding must be reached first." I might not understand, I thought, but I was riveted.

"Many time lines intersect here," she told me. "What has been shown you here in the Akashic, and in the crystal globe of eternity, all these are still but a fraction of what could be shown. But perhaps it will suffice to unveil for humanity how long and convoluted a history has been lived here on this small world.

"In the many Creations of Creator, a nearly infinite number of experiences unfold. If more specific information is needed, this will be given in time. For now this should suffice."

I asked if this information was to be included in the book She had told me to write.

"The book progresses and takes form." I guessed that meant *yes*.

"Truth is the essence, the center of being. There will be many moments coming when it will be tempting to substitute your own thoughts for Ours. This must never be allowed. You must be alert to temptation, for the dark force will seek to subvert Our words by discrediting you and all you write. Truth is your beacon and your hope of withstanding their attacks. You come to speak the Truth. The time is now and Truth must be your guide. We are with you in this way.

"The way in which you have written this history is acceptable to us with this exception: It is so rudimentary a history of the Truth that it is only a beginning. It is impossible to chronicle a linear history of Earth because much that has happened on the planet was not linear, but rather the result of interventions that altered the timeline."

I asked how on earth we poor mortals can ever hope to understand enough of Truth to succeed in finding enlightenment. She answered: "Avatars have been sent to your earthworld at critical times in history. Jeshua (Jesus) was one such."

Jeshua (Jesus)

"When One such as Jeshua incarnates, it is because humankind needs once again to have a beacon to follow. The Christed energy that he carries has such vast power that millions can be guided into the Light by it.

"The Christ energy is an expression of goodness and mercy. Many (Avatars) on your planet over the millennial past have expressed this energy in order to lead mankind out of the darkness that had been perpetuated against it.

Guruji had told me much the same thing about Lord Mahavir, the Jain Avatar, who incarnates every 2,000 years to teach truth. Needless to say, other cultures have memory of their own Avatars like Buddha and Krishna.

"As you know, the historical Jeshua and the Jesus Christ you were taught of in school were not the same."

The Mother explained this at length but it boils down to this; the Catholic Church purports to be the word of God, but it has, over the millennia, been run by human men whose motives were not always pure or benevolent and whose agendas regarding wealth and power tainted its teachings. By eliminating the female elements of God, Jesus' teachings of compassion and love were overwhelmed by power and the need to control.

"Jeshua traveled far and studied the Great Mysteries in order to bring Light into the world," She said. "He would have passed his teachings on to John and James and most especially to Mary of Magdala, called Miriam, but this was not allowed to happen.

"But like all the Light seeds planted here, his Light took root, and some have felt the truth that went far beyond churches or political agendas. His was a soul high and pure, but he was not the mythos created later to serve evil men in their evil purpose. You knew him well, in his earth life did you not?"

"I have always believed so." I had a memory of me as a small child seeking out Jesus in empty churches, as I never felt the vanilla picture of him I was given in religious classes matched the strong visceral picture of him I had in my Far Memory.

"Needless to say, Churches have used the name of this great Being for their own selfish needs. Sometimes there have been well-meaning blunders, more often there have been forces – dark forces – that saw in people's need to *believe*, an opportunity to control minds and hearts. Thus do heinous aberrations happen, like The Inquisition.

"Churches can do good work if they approach (humanity) with reverence, understanding and the compassion of the Christed Work. But their fatal flaw is that they interpose between humanity and God a fallible human source that is given credence as a conduit to The Divine. Many churches (different religions) exist because people came in to your planet at so many different stages of soul development – yet do they seek guidance toward the Light and so the churches sense this need and, at times, exploit it."

She said that much good and charitable work had been done over the centuries by those within (and outside of) churches – by people who sought to genuinely do the Christed work. But it was the hierarchical elements within the religions that had built empires, fortunes and political agendas, and had committed dreadful crimes against humanity, like Inquisition, pogroms and religious wars for their own agendas to amass power, wealth and control.

I was elated by Her mention of Jeshua/Jesus, as I'd always had a deep devotion to Him, and visceral far-memories of his earth life. I believed he had been far stronger and more dimensional than the Church had portrayed Him. Like the Church's view of Mother Mary and of Angels, Jesus had been watered down and altered to suit Church agendas. Inasmuch as it was nearly Christmas, I asked Mother to elaborate about the Truth of this divine emissary.

"You may write of the Light of the World on the event of this festival," She said. "Lord Jeshua carries the Light of the Universe, for it has been his task from time immemorial to enlighten the species who seek Light, as well as those who languish in darkness." She said there had been many others sent through time with this message of enlightenment for humanity, and that the Christed Energy had embodied in other guises throughout humanity's history to deliver this divine message when and where it was needed.

"He has worn many faces in many ages and eons. He has couched His message in many languages and ways, but always the message is *to the heart of the world*, and always it is the same: Love thy neighbor as thyself. Love God. Forgive as you would be forgiven. Seek the High Road, not the Low. Share what you have with those who have less.

"A simple message that carries within it all healing that is needed for your planet and its future. When the world vibrates to this frequency, then shall all doors be open and all secrets known. For the heart of the world is the heart of God/Goddess. And it is done."

"But it *isn't* done," I protested. "Man *doesn't* love his neighbor and wars rage all over the planet and man visits hideous atrocities on his fellow man."

"Jeshua/Jesus embodies all that can be known by humanity of love and kindness," She answered implacably. "He has said it in a thousand tongues and shown it in a thousand ways. He came to you as the embodiment of Truth and Love. His message has been used and twisted and changed by many whose agendas were served by this profaning of the sacred, but His Truth was so powerful and pervasive that it could be heard by the soul of humankind, even beneath the foolish trappings that profane men placed around it in an effort to serve their own purpose.

"His truth is transcendent for He is the Light of God embodied. His truth spreads still to those of all faiths who long to know God. His truth speaks still to the lonely and the suffering and the lost; even in the darkness, it resonates as a beacon of hope and possibility.

"Doubt not that He is the Christed One. Doubt not the Illumination He provides to a weary world. His Truth transcends and shall prevail.

"The festival of His birth is an ancient one and is not the time of his actual incarnation, but a time chosen for its resonance with His message. At the winter solstice, the celebration of new life to come out of the darkness of the fallow time was essential to the people, for it symbolized Hope and Rebirth. So, too, does the coming of this brave enlightenment come into the world of matter as a beacon and a hope for the future. In this time of celebration, in the name of all Holies that have graced your planet since the dawn of time, in the Name of the Light That Serves and The Light That Reigns, We send our blessing in the form of this message to the Heart of the World from the Heart of the Cosmos: Love one another. Forgive one another. Cherish the Earth and Her endless loving bounty. Speak the Truth. When in doubt about your actions, err on the side of kindness. You are loved and you are judged, but the Light of the Christ guides you on your arduous path.

"You may go now on this blessed day." (It was Christmas morning.) "Even the gods rejoice when a moment is achieved in the world of time and matter when love and truth are served and honored. It matters little that the message is diluted by those who seek to use a time of profound sanctity for commercial ends, because they who do such things do not understand that the deeper message still prevails. If for one night or one hour or one moment, humanity can resonate to the higher octave, it can do so again and again and again. It is as if a Celestial chord is struck and the note is heard on earth... a note so beautiful and sacred and profound that once heard, it can never be forgotten. Such a note was the Christed One. It was to carry this sound that He was born into the world of matter. And once the note is sounded, not all the darkness or chaos or anger or evil in the world can prevail against it. For the note has been heard and marked and remembered, and the collective soul of humankind has been called to hear.

"*Believe,* Alana, that the message to the Heart of the World cannot be stopped, cannot be contained, cannot be misused or misunderstood, for it is the Truth of the Heart of God and the note, once struck, can never be silenced.

"There is no need for intermediary between individuals and Creator. The connection made through prayer is genuine and completely real. There is no need for interpretation of God's essence, but at many stages of development there can be need of teaching, guidance and explanation. The purest path to Creator is through your (one's) own heart essence. Through love and meditative silence that allows the voice of Creator and his servants in the Light to be heard.

"Test all such leaders in the crucible of Christ Truth. If they have another agenda, if they seek power or money, if they fail to measure up to the selfless standard of the Christ, they are imposters who should not pretend to be his followers and his chosen teachers. Your soul recognizes the true ones and suspects the others. These suspicions are essential in your choice making. When in doubt, go directly to The Source. Remember, you need *no intermediary.* Speak directly from the heart. You (and all of us) will be heard and answered."

I asked how much of this world history my own soul had seen. Her reply stunned me.

"58,000 years as you count time," said The Mother, "has your soul been in this current process on planet earth. There was a time for you here before that as well, but it is not something to concern yourself with now."

If life on earth was a schoolroom, I guess nobody could accuse me of being a quick study! I burst out laughing, thinking of all the people I know in spiritual work who think they've completed the journey satisfactorily in one lifetime. I wondered what they'd say to how long I've been laboring here, without getting out of cosmic grade school.

"You have in truth known much, in your long soul history, Alana," Gaia said, reading my thoughts "as have others. But these truths are hard to retain, because the dark force sees the ones who carry the Light and sends great power against them. Power to subvert, to distort, and to cause forgetfulness." She said I was being given this material to disseminate in order to help others like me to remember.

CHAPTER 9

Creation

> *In the beginning was The Word. It sounded its vibratory frequency throughout space and will continue to sound until the dissolution. Sound creates time, which is merely a measurement to contain portions of infinite being. Time resides within and without. Just as light beams radiate out, so too do time lines radiate from a central nucleus of which there are an infinite number.*
>
> From the Mother's Teachings

Although the information here is redundant in part, I thought it was important enough to include in the Mother's own words:

"In the beginning Creator spoke the word of Creation and the sound vibration carried on it the potentiality of being for other lifeforms to come into beingness," the Great Mother told me one morning. "Creator's wish to experience determined this choice. Great beings were brought forth to serve Creator, these were the angels with whom you are so familiar. Other great beings of a different kind were brought forth as well. These you may call Godlings, for they were by your reckoning, capable of godlike feats and of great stature in the times in which they chose to be embodied.

"The free will, which Creator chose to allow, was the trigger point for diversity and differentiation. All was still within the heart/mind of Creator and all still remains. It is impossible for humans in their limitations to understand the scope of Creator or even of His/Her Creations, but a way must be found for you to tell this story so that humans and the others can comprehend it."

I asked if there is a beginning and an end to Creation or if it is infinite and eternal, as is Creator.

"Creation is an ongoing experience. There are an infinite number of Creations in progress and interactions among them are now, and have (always) been, commonplace. You seek to write a linear history of earth, but in truth no such history is possible because so many timelines and dimensions intersect.

"However, the history you have written which was inspired for the purpose of my book is acceptable. It touches on many points that are understandable to the human and it gives a framework, however frail and incomplete, to begin an understanding of some of the hidden mysteries of life.

"As the genome has begun to be understood, so now should history begin to be understood, although complete comprehension of either one by your primitive methods is not possible."

I told Her I was anxious for the history I was being given to be as complete as possible. It seemed to me we had been fooled and confused long enough.

"Be not afraid that your history is incorrect – it is merely incomplete. The one thing that should be clarified however is that there is a difference of species between angelic and human and hybrid – these differences are discernible to those with special sight but they will not be readily discernible to science for a long time to come.

"Be at peace with the history, we have given you. We inspire you not merely when We meet in the morning, but such inspiration can come at any time. You must however learn to differentiate so that you can live in Truth, never substituting your words for Ours. Be not afraid of that happening as We will help you to understand the difference with more clarity, as you become more adept at running the frequencies."

I said I understood and She continued.

"I would speak of the 4th and 5th Worlds today, to you. Beyond Atlantis, you draw nearer to your own time, so the story appears to be more complex and confusing to you.

"There are indeed new strains of children being born – part of an influx of souls with an altered vibratory field. They are not alone, however. Telepathic children, those who can access other realms with ease, will surface in abundance in this 5th World. Old species will mingle with the new, just as they have always mingled and communication will be altered substantially.

"The 4th World was one of tribal diaspora and of seeding life in many places on the planet. This life took many forms and the race consciousnesses that you currently perceive were a product of the five seedings. The stories you read in your biblical history are historical records, however inadequate, of one such people. Needless to say, the other survivors of the Great Flooding Time and other tribulations have their own record keeping, and as humankind had again reached the plateau of the written word, these records are in hidden repositories in several places.

They are also in legend and the spoken tradition, but these are couched in symbology and mythos so it becomes nearly impossible to trace truth. So much truth was the property of hidden initiates alone. What was spoken to the masses did not contain the keys to understanding; thus much ritual is meaningless except in the hands of initiates who hold the key (to unlock its power).

"To know the truth of history you would need to know the truth of all timelines and all dimensions of reality, thus what you now know is an outline, a framework for more learning... a beginning."

I asked The Mother if she is Creator. She said She is an emanation of Creator, but I saw a larger, older force behind Her and above Her as She spoke and knew She was showing me that She emanates from a Greater Source.

"You do not yet know how to correctly express the female principle of Deity," she explained. "This is a very difficult concept to comprehend while in the body, but nonetheless it is important that We clarify this issue for you."

(Other than the Jeshua presence I was so aware of, the three others who manifested to me in these dawn and dusk channelings were female. The Great Mother (I call her Isis) Gaia (the planetary intelligence), and Sipi Gualmo (the supreme deity of the Bon Po of Tibet), who is both the fierce protector and the compassionate Mother of her people. Until now, I'd always had difficulty understanding how Creator could manifest in so many forms and yet be One, so I welcomed any explanation She would offer.

"Creator and I are One Being," the Mother clarified. "The Manifestation of My Power – which embodies all female frequencies, sensibilities, noble-heartedness, maternalism, guardianship of home and hearth and all female sexuality, which is a force far more potent than your species understands at its current stage of development – is an embodiment of life force that is one half of the Empowerment that continuously creates and drives this universe, of which you are currently a part.

"As such, I am Co-Creator.

"Yet the Whole is greater than the sum of its parts. Thus Creator that embodies both male and female potentiality and being is beyond all. Yet this too, is but a small part of the story.

"Thus was I in existence before The Beginning. Thus will I be in existence beyond Time. Thus does all Truth dwell within me.

"Before language, before Time, before this Creation – and you are correct in suspecting the existence of other Creations – came into existence or potentiality of existence, *I AM*. When I choose to manifest for humanity's sake, I embody My Beingness in a form that can be comprehended by my vehicle to whom I manifest. Thus, what your third eye sees of Me is that which I permit to be seen of the Great Hologram, as you perceive it to be. A useful metaphor, by the way, for this stage of your development.

"More than this, you do not currently need to know. Truth is fearsome and so awe-inspiring as to render the servant useless for the tasks."

OK then, I thought as She spoke, it helps to know this much, at least.

PART III

My Life with the Unseen

CHAPTER 10

The Oneness of Creation

I had been pondering the concept of The Oneness of Creation for several days after the last transmission. I was beginning to understand the idea that Creator experiences life on our planet through each of us, but I wondered why an infinite intelligence would wish to do this. Why were individual lives really of interest to such an omnipotent and limitless Being? I asked the question: "Are we tiny ants of humans really of any consequence in the great scheme of things?"

"I will speak of The Great Oneness of Creation," was the reply, "and of the need to reinforce your own sense of the importance of individual human life within the Celestial Oneness. Each soul essence, although part of the far greater oversoul as it has been called, is also utterly unique in its manifestation of life energy. Each "ant" as you termed it, each "atom" that is an individual, plays out a role and destiny that is absolutely unique in the history of Creation. As the Creator of Essence of the Universal Oneness experiences Itself through each individual, it experiences a new and utterly unique manifestation. While this may seem small in the great scheme of billions and mega-billions of soul essences within the Oneness, yet it is like no other and it is part of Creator. As your eyes and arms and legs are part of you and so essential to your wholeness, and every cell has its purpose, so are you essential to Creator.

"The Great Oneness experiences you as you experience life. You are eternal life as It is. You play out your role in this life and many others within the infinite confines of The Oneness. A lovely paradox, is it not?"

A cosmic bafflement seemed a better description to me and I said so.

"Within the Oneness are the many. Humans, angels, beings you could not dream [of]. The vastness of the Oneness makes It inaccessible to finite lives, but not to the soul, which, too, is infinite. So within the Celestial Oneness there are a vast number of stratifications of beingness, hierarchical and complex, that constitute a reality with which the limited parts of you can cope – Angels, Gods, Goddesses, fellow humans, animals, insects, bacteria and all the other individual manifestations of life.

"You cannot understand it in the limited state of humanness. You cannot because you do not have the capacity to enfold within your mind the infinite complexities. This is as it should be. Do not strive for that which is impossible and would be of no use to you in earth life.

"Yet it is important that you not lose sight of the importance of each individual life. None goes unheeded. None is less important than the next. Within the Oneness all are not equal, but they are beloved."

That was interesting! Reading my mind the Mother added,

"They are not equal except on a soul level where they are equal indeed, and of more consequence than you know.

"You were correct in your vision of the Great Hologram that is The Oneness. You are contained within and are One with It."

"I'm trying to understand, Mother," I said, "but this isn't easy."

"I take the time to elaborate because when humans access The Oneness they feel, often, that in their smallness within The Vastness, they are of no consequence. This is not the case. *All* develops as *each* develops."

I then asked, "Are you, too, then, part of The Hologram, but at an infinitely higher level, Mother?"

"I AM the Hologram. This is not a teaching you can currently comprehend. Look to the Wisdom Stone (to be described in Book II), not for understanding of this concept, but for comfort with your place in The Plan."

"So there is a Plan?," I asked, perking up.

"There is *more* than a Plan, there is Purpose. All is as it should be. All is unfolding as it should. Do not trouble yourself with that which does not concern you. Within the finite confines of your current reality, proceed in truth and all will be as it should be and must be."

I suddenly felt very vulnerable and inadequate for the responsibility of carrying the Message. I asked if I could fail in the task of messenger because I wasn't able to comprehend all the complexities of the message.

"When a human vehicle is carrying the Message of a Deity or a Divine Command, they can fail as a human, but not as a Messenger," was the answer I was given. "Human frailties – selfishness, unconsciousness, ignorance, venality, and a host of other possibilities still exist for the entity, in whatever degree has been reached by that particular soul. Only when the entity speaks for the Divine is there infallibility."

That one idea startled me because I'd always laughed at the hubris of the Pope who had declared himself infallible in 1872, granting all Popes who followed similar status. I wondered how that meshed with this teaching, but didn't have time to ask before She continued,

"Only the Direct Transmission has the potential to be unflawed. Humans seek perfection in the vessel, but this is unrealistic. The vessels themselves seek this perfection in themselves, as they strive to measure up to the standards set by their gift of soul. This does not mean they will not or cannot fail – it simply means they *strive* to be a worthy vessel whether they reach the goal or not. You will be reprimanded when you fail, just as you are frequently told when you do not. On occasion, like this day, We will choose to remind you of an obligation."

I thought of all the famed Gurus who had left great teachings behind, but were seriously flawed as human beings. How could we humans sort out where the divinity ended and the flaws began?

PART IV

Cleveland On Tuesday

CHAPTER 11

Free Will

The obvious next question, it seemed to me, was this:

How much freedom do we really have to make these all-important choices? Having been raised an Irish Catholic, and having become an Astrologer, the question of free will has troubled me all my life. Is most of life already pre-ordained and therefore beyond our choice making? Does God really want us to surrender our free will to Him/Her as many churches and Oprah suggest, or is that just the ultimate cop-out and a good way to leave all choice-making in the hands of intermediaries like priests and ministers? Just how much say-so do we have at all those hundreds of everyday crossroads we're faced with?

I asked the Mothers to give me help with this thorny issue.

"The concept of surrendering the Will to God/Goddess," said the Great Mother, "is misunderstood on your planet. It grieves Us to see the ways in which it is misused as a concept, for the most part in good will and earnestness by those who wish to serve, but in cold-hearted manipulation by those who wish to prosper in religions that have long since lost their faith, their connection to Deity and their good will toward humanity.

"Your own ambivalence toward this concept for a lifetime has been a perfect study. You believe you are to do it all as best you can and then lay the result upon the altar. (Taking responsibility for the results and suffering the consequences.) At the same time a small voice urges you to surrender all will and let what happens, happen.

"Neither is correct.

"In giving free will to your species, We intended the evolution of consciousness and of soul. We set up guideposts in the Universe and from time to time sent Avatars to reinforce the pure thought and will of Deity made manifest in mortal form, in order to make the teachings more accessible.

"It was never intended that an individual lay down his own will, awaiting Our whims and pleasures. In doing so, no soul progress can be made. Nor was it intended that an individual shoulder all burdens alone, slugging through the minefields of the human condition, only to present to Us at the end of an embodiment, a bloody, battered and beleaguered soul that has survived the slings and arrows of the human condition, but was unable to accomplish much because of all the trials endured. Mind you, when such does come before Us, We are quite cognizant of the purity of intent that drove said soul to such a difficult incarnation, and often such humans have made vast strides of soul by having lived their lives thus."

"So what exactly do you expect of us, then?" I asked exasperated and still confused.

"This, then, is what We had in mind, eons ago, when first the course was prepared and humanity unleashed to begin its climb, its return to Godhead and its ultimate triumphal reconnection with Creator," She replied ignoring my attitude.

"To be aware of Our laws that transcend those of humanity. To love and respect Us and to love and respect each other. To do no harm to other sentient beings. To be shepherds of the many extraordinary species We created to enhance your journey. To guard the exquisite home-world you were entrusted with, and to enjoy its fruits without plundering, destroying or making it uninhabitable. To grow in Truth and Love. To create more, to go beyond, to strive to know, to strive to be all of what We gave you the potential to be. To touch the stars, not to own them, but to enter the full realm of consciousness of your Universe. To share with all life forms and in doing so, learn more of Who We Are Who Formed You.

"So, what do we ask of you who struggle? We ask that you love and respect Us and yourselves. That you exercise your will to enhance and grow toward Us. That you surrender to the Greater Whole, the Higher Concept, the Ultimate Truth, which is Love and Truth combined."

It reminded me of a conversation I'd had years ago with a wonderful metaphysician named Eleanor Wrench. When I questioned her about the subject of free will, she said in a very kindly manner, "Let me explain it to you, dear. If God wants you in Cleveland on Tuesday, you have the free will to get there by foot, train or car. But believe me, Cathy, you will be in Cleveland on Tuesday."

CHAPTER 12

Humanity and Free Will

I was still not satisfied that I understood how much control or not we have over our destiny. Books like *The Secret* (which was published later, but had many similar predecessors) claim we have the powers of Gods to control fate, but I hadn't seen any evidence of that. So, I asked again how much of our reality we create and how much is inevitable.

"Within the Hologram that is God/Goddess/Creator and created, all powers exist for all. It is true that you hold the power of creation just as Deity does but many reasons and obstacles keep mortals from exercising this power. Imagine the chaos if every human on planet Earth, and every being on every other world was fully in charge of this power and was, at every given moment, creating worlds anew. Therefore certain restrictions and limitations exist in each of the nearly infinite realms of experience Creator has chosen to experience with you and others.

"Creator experiences Creation on a moment to moment continuum with those that He/She has brought into being. Within the context of that exponential wholeness, an infinite variety of possibilities and probabilities exist.

"Each individual soul that is part of the essence of the Godhead has been sent forth upon the journey to create, to learn, to feel, to become all it can before its ultimate return to Source.

"During the multiple lifetimes – and your soul, dear priestess, is nearing the end of your earthly sojourn so I will tell you now that the thousands of lives you've lived have brought you to this moment of revelation and not for the first time. When you served me in the past and in certain times in which you served other manifestations of deity, you understood full well how the continuum works. You have traversed the Universe and seen much not shown to most mortals, and you store this important knowledge in a physical way within the hippocampuses of your brain, but in a larger way, within your soul essence.

"But on your journey, as happens in earth incarnations, you have faltered and blundered as well as soared. You have had to experience certain deep emotions that cannot be imagined or synthesized. The chief of these that I will discuss today is sorrow.

"For many lifetimes you have carried a vast burden of sorrow within your cellular memory. Sorrow, suffering, illness, pain. You have sought the truth and spoken it and you have died endless deaths in its service. This is the lifetime in which you come to serve in a new way before you leave the earthplane entirely.

"In order to so serve, you have been once again thrust into The Crucible. Fear, the dominant emotion on this planet had to be experienced to the fullest and vanquished. Illness, pain, suffering, loss – all these were reprised in your life so that you – an empath – could understand these vibrations in a singular way and help to transmute them for humanity.

"Therefore, in answer to your question, yes, you have created your reality, but not in the negative way in which you have understood the equation. What was placed in your path was a learning course in which skills could be redeveloped. Having survived The Crucible and developed the skills, you may now access Deity in a different way and create a different kind of life.

"So just as illness is not a simple matter of *thinking* it away, and yet the mind does have great power over it, so you can create now, that which you could not create before in all areas of your life.

"This initiation has led you to great learning and will give you singular Power to help others and to teach what you have learned.

"You may now receive what you need and wish from the Universe in abundant prosperity. You may now disseminate the Message.

"Your newfound ability to create in a new and positive way will bring benevolence to you and to many. Believe in Me. Believe that I work through you. Believe in your power to create, for you are part of Me and The Mothers, and we choose to work through you.

"Stay in truth. Stay in love. Stay in joy and understanding. Share all we teach except for that which must remain secret. Be one with us and believe we will provide for you and Vraya. And for many."

CHAPTER 13

The DNA of Humans

If so many of us are hybrids, what exactly constitutes humanity, I asked one day? The answer was fascinating but still left me with questions.

"I will speak of the 12 strands of DNA that were original to your species. As you were conceived by Creator, you were to function as effortlessly as the speed of thought. You were a Light body that was part of the Source, and this primordial Light body had been gifted with a new capacity for sensory perception, manifest in the material world as a material body. For eons of time as you understand it, you were in the process of incorporating into your species the combined abilities of both the light body and the material body. The material encryption was written in your DNA, which is in itself an encryption-based system meant to be used for the purpose of experimentation with the potentials of the species."

So we are computer-like, I thought. I've wondered since, if that's why our newest generation of children are able to exist in cyberspace as much as in the material world. I wonder if the next evolution we'll experience will be a return to telepathy.

"As the species evolved, intermarried, devolved from spirit and attunement with The One, and as interventions and interferences occurred, your encoding altered. This alteration was sometimes evolutionary accident and sometimes specific programming of those whose agendas were better served by your enslavement.

"Accessment of the higher coding of 12 strand DNA makes communication with the Source far easier and more viable. Feats of mind and body become possible that were known to only a few of your species over the ages, the avatars and enlightened Beings who had grown beyond material substance and in conquering matter had reestablished the energy patterning of your original code.

"Many strive for this now, as 4th Dimensional and 5th Dimensional consciousness nears for many. Your own alteration has been part of this plan. What those who strive must understand is that going to a class or learning a process, or paying money to a Master, is not sufficient unto this task. The entire *being* must seek alteration and reconnection with Source. Implants (intentional impediments) must be sought actively and removed. Spiritual legwork must be done. Enslavements of varied sorts must be left behind. The goal is great, but the path is rigorous."

I still wanted to know just how much our actions affect our fate. The idea that we can create our own reality as if we were Gods seemed pretty implausible to me, yet a lot of New Age teaching was headed in that direction. The subject came up one morning without my needing to ask.

"We would speak of your co-creation of your life," the Mother said, "This is a concept that is misunderstood and misused more often than not.

"To tell a human or human hybrid that he/she is co-creator with God is to tell a half-truth. It is obvious to all that The Omniscience and Omnipotence of God is far beyond human powers. Therefore, for the most part, when faced with this statement, the human feels inadequate and short-changed. He/She is shocked that all that has been seen in life contradicts the possibility of this being so. So where lies the truth?

"You are each molecular energy in constant motion. The molecular energy that you are is part of a larger molecular energy truth. I speak here in simplistic terms that you may comprehend My words. In a higher sense, the very concept of molecules is puerile, but for now, for this teaching, it will do.

"Your thoughtforms carry a powerful electrical charge – powerful enough to alter the dance of your molecular structure. In heroic deeds, in athletic feats, in inspired moments of speech, as your thought energy impacts your molecular field, changes occur in what you perceive to be reality. Some miracles are due to divine or angelic intervention, some are due to the change in electromagnetic fields I have just described.

"Therefore, it is true that you have the capacity to alter the reality around you. If you hold the thought of overweight (an issue you currently wrestle with), your body will find a way to keep you overweight against all laws of biology. If you can successfully change the thought form of yourself to hold an image of perfect weight, your body will accommodate this picture.

"Where you and the Gods differ is that for you to hold such an altered picture is a difficult task. Karma, past life experience, current life experience, parental admonishment, societal pressure to conform, and genetic patterning brought from the ancestral gene pool, all continue to keep your thought form locked into a certain reality. To explode free of this and substitute a new reality is no easy task. It is, however, possible.

"These concepts are not easy ones for your species at this moment in time/space, but they are understandable if explained thus. You are so often victims of programming far beyond your ken. We seek to expose the programs and to expunge their pervasive poisons. We seek to help you fight your way to freedom from control.

"So the power to co-create exists within you, but you must fight your own thought forms as well as those imposed on you, to do it.

"For the next week, you are instructed to think only of perfect health and a perfect body. Let no other image intrude. We will discuss this again after one week's time, as you count time. You may be quite surprised by your observations."

A week or so later, I awakened from a vivid dream, probably prompted by my pondering all that had been said about our ability to alter our own destiny. I woke up wanting to know about what choices are available to us in following the path already seemingly laid out for us, so I asked very pointedly for answers.

Oneness

"Universal Mind is the mind of God in a great many ways," the Mother answered me. "If the mind is thought of as the intelligence behind action, then this metaphor applies. The Mind of God the Highest is so far beyond the comprehension of earth's beings that it is almost ludicrous for a human to contemplate this issue, but it is understandable that they do so, and so I shall attempt to clarify an answer to the question that awakened you.

"The Universal Flow, the Universal Mind that is accessed by some beings on a continuing basis, and by humans on an occasional basis, is a part of the great Oneness. All minds can be accessed, all time space, all places that exist in matter, and most which exist in non-matter can be thus accessed.

"When a human reaches into the Flow and is carried on its multi-frequency tide, that human feels Godlike because she/he can hear/see/think/ experience/participate in/explore/and to a degree, comprehend, a larger truth than the one usually available to his/her consciousness, which is small and finite. In touching a more infinite reality, it appears that person has touched the essence of All That Is. This is not quite the case, but it is sufficiently close in truth to be useful as a working model for us today.

"You humans are free to go to the Flow. Free to interact with others. The admonition not to interfere with someone else's life is a good one, as much karma can be incurred by such meddling with another's soul journey. As to creating riches and power, this is quite acceptable if it is done with correct intent, which is not to take what belongs to others, but to call forth that which is your own in the Universe, which is often considerable accumulation. No harm attends your soul in so asking for that which is yours.

"Similarly, you may ask for health, but your soul will choose its own lessons and may not respond in the way you imagine. Work can be accessed, love, friendship, many fulfillments are possible by accessing the Flow of 'Universal Current,' if you will.

"But none of what I have described makes a human into a God, despite what your "New Agers" believe and some scientists posit.

"Work with this concept in the days to come, and then we will again speak of it.

"You have had many indications of late that We speak the truth to you, no matter how implausible."

That was true. Also disconcerting.

It was just another way of saying 'Cleveland on Tuesday.'

CHAPTER 14

The Manipulation of Truth

"We will speak today of *Truth and Love and Compassion*," the Mother said one November morning, "for in this time these concepts are no longer held by many to be the way, and yet they are the surest, fastest, most direct route, not only to Us, the Celestials, who guard and guide you, but to the salvation your world is now in such dire need of.

"The endless manipulation of Truth, by governments, by corporations, by those whose job it is to recreate fact for the masses – this has created (and will create) confusion of such magnitude that Truth no longer occupies the place it must in your hearts as a species.

"Were you to see Truth itself within your own matrix, you would see a brilliant pillar of golden light that stretches from the Truth of Us through the

Crown, to the Heartseed thence downward, where it then goes interdimensional, so that at this stage of your understanding you would not discern its destination other than to know it no longer is confined to your material world, but transcends the boundaries imposed upon your world.

"Its journey to and through the heart is essential to the proper functioning of the heart chakra itself. The heart, which is, as you know the conduit to Us, is fed celestial energy by this golden mein of Truth, nourished by its capacity to connect worlds in an appropriate and energetically nourishing way.

"The more a human lies or equivocates in the course of a life, the farther off center this golden energy conduit becomes. It shrivels, losing its capacity to carry divine light from Source to Source. The human strays from The Path, The Source and The Light. Lies become the coin with which he pays for what he receives... the more he denies the Light in this manner, the closer he comes to the opposite polarity. A gradual endarkenment suffuses the being and his capacity to reach Us is diminished in significant ways.

"The energetic pathway of Truth carries a specific frequency – that frequency accesses our aid with ease. When *Truth* frequency meets *Love* frequency, so that Truth is spoken not as a weapon but as a tool of compassion, then does the mortal reach the closest to Our Divinity and the closest to what we intended in The Beginning.

"When a mortal serves his fellow men and women in Truth, Love and Compassion, he lives in a state of Divine Perfection and fulfillment. The length of time in which he remains in this ecstatic state will vary, but the soul expands exponentially in such a state and old karma falls away like dust before the hurricane.

"Truth, Love, Compassion are what you seek as a species from Creator and His minions sent to guide you. Does it not make sense that We seek the same from you? Teachings will come to you in ways that will express this viscerally."

"This issue of Truth is of great consequence, I can see that," I answered, disturbed suddenly by the fact that by being in the advertising business, which is built on spin-doctoring the truth to the advantage of the client, I'd inadvertently contributed to this erosion of people's ability to separate Truth from lie. I started a quick mental inventory of old clients but was interrupted.

"Truth prevails over all," The Mother reiterated. "Each must answer for his own. The door to the Center, to Deity, to the World soul, to the Soul itself – all these depend upon the Golden Cord of Truth.

When you equivocate, you are not on center. When you make life easy for someone at the expense of truth, you are not on center. When you speak from the heart place and from the Celestial, your center resonates with a light and sound that is in harmony with the divine sound, and you secure your path.

"Truth is essential. Truth has been lost and abused on your world. It must be restored. The truth is bent and battered and twisted, so that children grow believing lies are acceptable, believing that heinous deeds can be done to this planet and to humanity and then lied about, making them acceptable.

"In your current world in which each must fight for survival, truth has become mitigated by circumstance. Humans lie to live – lie to their employer, to their spouses, to their children, even to themselves. The greater the chaos and darkness on the planet, the more they feel the need to lie. The more they lie, the greater the chaos and darkness. Yet, Truth and Love are the two vibratory frequencies that can set you free. Free to vibrate with the Gods, and to tap their essence, for it is your own as well."

Truth and Love... it suddenly occurred to me that these two energies were probably the least understood, the most misused, and the most unlikely to go hand-in-hand, particularly when the madness of sexual attraction takes over our body/minds. I said as much but the answer was oblique.

"The new Babies of Light are arriving on this homeworld from others. They are volunteers, as is Vraya. They come with a clear understanding of truth. The golden cord that connects to the High Self is strong in them.

"They will withstand the equivocation of their elders and they will restore truth to the planet. Giant corporations like (she named several shockingly familiar names) are the rapists of your homeworld. They abuse the indigenous, they steal the earth's treasures, they genetically engineer seeds to lose their life force, and they change the matrix of food so it no longer nourishes. They lie to all about their motives. They must be exposed and stopped.

"This war for your planet is ages old and will continue for a time. Your job is not this. Your job is to open the door to enlightenment for many.

"So much of beauty has been given to your people, mortal. And yet they have wreaked havoc."

That was true as far as it went, but I didn't think it was a fair rebuke.

"But my people have been kept ignorant of all these truths, Mother," I argued. "They have been taught lies. This hasn't helped them to know how or what to believe. I don't make excuses for our wrongdoing, I only make the case that it feels to me that Truth told at this time will help us do better. I only wish it had happened sooner!"

"This is correct and appropriate thinking. I applaud it, for this is why I speak directly now. The record must be cleared and set straight.

"The information that was given to you about the wavelength of love vs. the wavelength of fear/anger, etc. is quite correct. Truth too, has a wavelength. The wavelength of truth and that of universal love are similar. They both communicate directly to The Divine and align the energy bodies with Divine Source.

"Truth is a golden cord that stretches up to the Celestial from the interdimensional seed atom (of the heart), just as the cord that you originally saw when you traveled to the Celestial, does. Now that you understand the holographic nature of the universe, you no longer need to see the cord, yet it remains, if needed.

"When you vibrate at the rate of perfect truth, without equivocation, you generate a field that accesses the Divine and allows access to Divine Power. When it was spoken, *'And the Truth shall set you free,"* this was the meaning.

"To love is to vibrate. To catch (the vibratory rate of) this frequency, think of the most love-filled moments of your life and hold the pulsation. In your case, Dakota, your father and sister, are the places to look in your current life history for a sense of this vibratory frequency."

Chastened by the Truth

That evening I returned for another round at dusk. The way the session ended still makes me laugh at the memory.

"The teaching continues about Truth and the soul's journey toward completion," The Mother said without preamble.

"Truth is like a homing beacon. It goes directly to the Celestial Realm and resonates there. Equivocation and untruth vibrate at far lower frequencies.

"When the soul gets in the habit of getting by with less than Truth, the potential for a given lifetime lowers and lowers until the person's path narrows and is confined to mundane existence.

"When Truth is the central attitude of a person's being, doors and windows open continuously to the Celestial. Miracles, angels (appear), opportunities for rapid soul growth happen. Sometimes the opportunities are hardships and difficulties, and then after, both the native and the world assume that this person has done something very wrong to deserve such a fate. Quite the opposite may be true. The choice of expiating Karma is a time-shortening device in the life of the soul and a blessing.

"As a soul nears completion of an earth cycle, much karma seems to hit time after time after time, and the person grows weary and often angry at fate. But often it is at this very moment that he or she is most blessed."

I wasn't happy with this cavalier view of suffering.

"Why must life be so hard, Mother?" I asked. "I see others who seem to skim through life happy, prosperous and protected. Why is my life so hard?"

She answered evenly and didn't chide me for my petulance.

"Some are not awake yet, some are being given a reward lifetime, and some are unwilling to start the climb or to serve," she told me, then added matter-of-factly, "All must eventually meet the Lords of Karma."

That sounded fairer, but still not so great. I wasn't giving up so easily.

"Is getting off the Wheel of Earth Reincarnation a good thing, Mother? Or do we just go to another wheel and another? Until our souls are too exhausted to go on?"

She sounded benevolent in answering.

"Earth time is the hardest. All other realms have the blessings of telepathy and bodiless movement at the speed of thought. Most find that agreeable. At higher levels there is higher awareness of the gods and of Creator. Oneness with Creator is the final reward.

"I have so many questions, Mother," I persisted, looking at my watch and remembering I had a date to get ready for. This one time, I had chosen to channel at dusk and now time was fleeting.

The Mother read my mind and offered an unsought bit of information.

"The man who comes to visit is not your soul mate, but he is decent and will be attracted to you. Keep a level head."

I burst out laughing. This was a truth to be paid attention to!

CHAPTER 15

Love. The Heart of the Matter

One beautiful summer morning I was greeted with The Mother's promise to teach me about Love, a heady subject and one that intrigued me on so many levels: I hadn't been lucky in love when it came to spouses, but I had been greatly blessed by love of family and friends, so I was anxious to know more.

"Love is the essence of universal life force," The Mother said. "It empowers and generates, but it is quite different from your perception of it and We wish to clarify for you what universal love demands of you."

It seemed she was speaking not of the love between couples, but of love as a state of being.

"Love is an energy frequency that you (humans) must learn to access. Once understood on a soul level, it can be used to radiate outwards in an ever-widening circle and band that can transmute all in its path.

"It does not mean that you are to give of yourself indiscriminately, or without conscious thought. It does not mean that you do not discern those who help and those who harm. Quite the contrary, it means that you must make these choices in your immediate circle, but you must, on a broader scale, make allowance for humanity's frailty.

"You did not understand frailty and had to be shown your own, in ways that seemed cruel and punishing. You were arrogant in your faith, although you did not intend to be thus, but had not been tested fully in this lifetime." Sadly, I realized this was true. I had thought I'd always be protected from harm because of my faith in God, but I had learned and paid deeply for the learning, that faith tests us sorely and many have suffered and died for it. I was naïve and hopelessly romantic and idealistic about love, but lived to learn the foolishness of following the heart alone, instead of heart and head in equal measure.

"You did not see your flaws and now you do. This is progress. Although to you it seems grave pain."

"Mother, I mean no disrespect," I said, both hurt and concerned, "but it seems to me we humans are created flawed and then suffer and are punished for being flawed. What's the point of that?"

"It is a great Mystery," She responded, unhelpfully. "You will understand when you are no longer flawed."

I guess I don't have to tell you how pointless *that* seemed to me. I nearly laughed out loud.

But then, taking pity on me, I think, She went on to say that I must share the message of love's power as a counterweight to greed and cruelty, and that by writing about it, I could become a conduit for Divine Love to help humanity. If that could be the case, I guessed it would supersede my flaws, which were apparently more abundant than I'd ever imagined.

"Humanity must establish the link to its own heart core energy," she went on, "to the seeds of compassion, to the power of forgiveness, to the majesty of love. In so doing, those who cannot connect intellectually with the concept of the Divine will connect with the *essence* of the Divine. The wave will begin as a pebble dropped in a pool radiates a small and gentle eddy about it, and then it will grow to tidal proportion. People will seek opportunities to love as they now seek opportunities to take and to hoard. A great wave of goodness and mercy will be begun that is inexorable, unstoppable in its might and power.

People will open the floodgates of the heart to each other, and in so doing, the (Earth) Mother Intelligence, who is The Great Mother of this planetary energy field, will be healed as her children are healed.

"The power of love is inexorable. The power of love and truth *combined* can change your world in ways you cannot dream. The frequency band of love/truth will reconnect the family of humanity to its roots in the Divine. There is still time to act. There is still time for redemption. There is still time for the spirit of Groundswell to alter the course of the future.

"Goodness carries replenishment in its field. Compassion, mercy, kindness, all the attributes of love, carry with them the cosmic payback that humanity seeks now with all the yearnings of its soul. Your species longs for grace, longs for love, longs for fulfillment, and longs to fill the empty places within that greed has not filled."

Amen to *that*, Mother.

CHAPTER 16

Love/Sex/Relationship

My divorce had been devastating, the reality of betrayal a wound I found very hard to heal. It wasn't merely that I didn't trust men, but that I no longer trusted my own judgment. I had been so terribly fooled and suffered so gravely for it, I was loathe to open my heart to the possibility of such wounding ever again.

I longed to understand more about love, sex, the truth of men and women's relationships and why we seem destined for more heartache than happiness in this crucial part of life. I asked the Mother to help me understand. The answer was more than a little surprising. I think it would have made me laugh, if it didn't touch on so much unhappiness in human relationships.

"When humans split into the two consciousnesses of male and female, a dynamic was set up not merely to procreate as your science believes, but to allow Creator to experience life intimately through each consciousness. The consciousnesses were far closer soon after the split than they are now, for the telepathic understanding of each one's need was clearly defined for the other. Male saw female and not only desired her physically, but he longed for the comfort of her spirit and the wholeness he experienced in her presence. Female similarly longed for the completeness she had enjoyed before the split. She longed to rejoin, to reconnect and to re-experience the security that had been lost to her.

"Because Creator divided the beingness/beings in such a way that the polarities of universal energetics were to be served, certain true differences were necessary in order to create the energetic spark that would power all else. Thus, the two were not formed to blend again into perfect peaceful connectedness, but rather were engineered to *challenge each other* and to create *a network of tensions* that would have to be overcome in order for harmony to be achieved and the energetics to be served."

A network of tensions... *that* explained a lot.

"Over the millennia the differences have escalated, each side drawing further into its own sphere of being, its own camp, if you will. Rather than bridging the gap with a dynamic force field generated by the interaction that was possible, men and women have become so disappointed in each other's inadequacies that harmony is seldom achieved, except early in a relationship when the sexual explosiveness bridges the energy gap with a powerful burst of connective energy – a molecular blending that gives people a great, if momentary, glimpse of what life was like in the beginning of time as you know it.

"How you ask, can man and woman ever bring each other lasting peace and joy? There are some who achieve this bliss, some whose souls remember the pathways that create challenge enough to power passion, yet allow the spiritual bond to become so strong that both partners are empowered by it and larger than they would be if separated.

"Karma plays a role as well, for the partnership of marriage permits an enclosed circle in which many lessons can be learned and those who come together are often not meant to engender bliss and harmony for each other, but quite the opposite. Sex forms the attraction that permits the play to begin, the soul then uses the opportunities and stresses to play out its grand design."

I must have looked as glum as I felt about this information.

"Your heart is made heavy by these truths for you still remember your soulmate from the early days (of my soul journey through eons) and the loyalty you carry as a soul entity causes you to long to re-experience with him the time of connectedness.

"There are some for whom this is reality in a given lifetime. For most it is not. What can be achieved with effort is a mutual respect for the different gifts of the opposite gender. And depending on the development of the individual soul, there can be genuine love. But this phenomenon is rare, not ordinary, and can only be achieved with care, patience and mutual willingness to truly understand the truths of the other's need and desire to fulfill those needs as non-judgmentally as possible."

"There must be equality of giving and receiving – this is so seldom managed in your species for hurts are hoarded and eventually express themselves in varied acts of betrayal.

"Love is a far more complex issue between the genders than we can complete today. There are experiences yet to come for you that will clarify the essences of male and female. This is enough for now."

"It all seems so sad and unfulfilling for both, Mother," I said, meaning it.

"In many ways, daughter, this is Truth as well. But there is more we will explore another day that will unfold more of Creator's plan in this regard."

CHAPTER 17

The Other Side of Love... Women and Divorce

One of my students, who was also a karate sparring partner, was a lawyer-turned-Swami, who specialized in helping women and children in abusive relationships. She asked me to ask a question of the Mothers about something that troubled her deeply. She wondered why women are exploited in so many places in the world and how to help those who had been so broken by divorce and betrayal that they seemed unable to recover.

"There is a lesson in universal energies that is difficult but essential for women to learn," was the surprising reply when I asked the first question.

"Your (women's) throats are directly connected energetically to your genitals. You must learn to open your throats to speak your woman truths in order to free your sexual natures." (This statement reminded me of the admonition so well written in *Women Who Run with Wolves*.)

"You (women) close your throats in order to keep the peace with your beloveds. In so doing you too often shut your throats *and* your loins. You must free the whole Conception Vessel (this is a Chinese concept – a meridian that powers female sexuality and strength) and try to free your vision of self in order to raise kundalini energies and be who you are meant to be. Fierce, wholly sexual female nature has frightened men for millennia. They (men) feel a desperate need to subjugate what they fear. So women have been changed in shape, clothing, demeanor, etc. to meet their specifications. Second-class and malleable. Women have been complicitous in this to achieve the protection of men in a male dominant world.

"Now women can and must break free. The Goddess energy will flow in, in times to come, to make the female energies whole again.

"There are energies of receptivity that must be kept open and active in a woman in order for her to be able to receive love, money, help. There will be further teachings from this Source, but for now this vast concept is one which requires attention, meditation and detailed discussion as to the methodology for helping women to re-experience openness."

Needless to say, I asked to know more.

"The key lies in forgiveness and love on a level of frequency," the Mother said. "Both forgiveness and love are extraordinarily difficult energies to reinstate when a woman is in a state of woundedness. Concentrate on this issue and pray for inspiration. Talk to women who have been so wounded and sift through their responses to your questions for the glimmer of gold amidst the sordid debris. From the women's suffering itself, their deliverance will come, but the road is fog-bound for them in their suffering and many wrong turns are taken before clarity is reached. The energetic understanding of their plight can speed the process, but you must be guided in the means of guiding others. Your intention is correct, so you will be given help.

I asked the second of Grace's questions:

"As to the exploitation of the female of your species: Before balance is found there is imbalance. The male energies have dominated your planet for nearly four thousand years. This was not always so, and as our Messenger can attest from all that we have told her of this Truth, the time is now upon you of a shift in Universal energy toward the female once again.

"In an epoch of male dominance the female is used, vilified, exploited and ridiculed. Male strengths are applauded, female strengths are denigrated. When this consciousness reaches its apex – which is just before its collapse and decline – the plight of some can be very sad and they can feel great helplessness.

"As the tide changes and female energies flood in from Celestial Sources, perception alters. Women's healing powers, intuition, psychic gifts, nurturance and capacity for deep emotional understanding are again given credence and their value is perceived. Needless to say, the test then becomes one of whether the oppressed then becomes the oppressor, or instead, in conscience and generosity offers to find a middle road in which the strengths of each half of your species are respected and made use of in constructive ways.

"When the exploited becomes the exploiter, an endless downward cycle of destruction is maintained. Only when one half raises the bar and allows the other half its due is The Whole served and advanced. (*Note:* Strangely, this paragraph was given to me to add after the rest, as if to make the point singularly clear.)

"Each soul in its journey wears the trappings of male and the trappings of female in varied lifetimes. By experiencing the extremes of bliss and degradation and all that lies between, the soul expands experientially and eventually finds its way to a place in which it could never countenance exploiting another, because on a deep soul level it carries the memory of the pain of such exploitation.

"For eons your species has see-sawed through male dominant and female dominant times in which the excesses of each have remained imbalanced. Only when you reach a place of using the best of the Celestial energetic influx of power to come to a respectful balance will this see-saw effect be mitigated.

"This planetary test has been failed in many occasions, sometimes so badly that great cataclysmic decimations are the legacy of this selfishness and foolhardiness. Each half of your species carries a message of strength and passion and opportunity from The Celestial. In balance, your species can reach the next plateau of consciousness. In exploitation, this achievement can never be reached."

"If all this is so," I asked, "how can it be altered in everyone's best interest?"

"You seek to mitigate suffering," she answered. "To do so you must educate to Truth. If women now merely retaliate against their aggressors and exploiters, the dance continues. If they can use the Universal female energy to expand into forgiveness, love and a mutual raising of the standard of behavior, the next dimension of consciousness awaits.

"The choice, as always, lies within."

CHAPTER 18

Love Vibration

"There is a guarded teaching about the love vibration that we would have you access now," Mother said. That sounded intriguing. A guarded teaching... wonder what that means?

"The wavelength of love is intensely powerful," She said and I almost said *duh!* but managed to contain myself. "In fact, it is the most powerful you can reach in a mortal body. It is dreadfully misunderstood and confused with sexuality, which sometimes accompanies it.

"The love vibration is felt most strongly and purely in the mother/child bond, which produces a wavelength that moves mountains. This wavelength is larger and stronger than you think, for it not only makes your heart beat rapidly but makes remarkable strengths accessible.

"To remain in the love energy band is difficult, but once achieved it connects to the Divine and permits Divine Powers to flow. Because humans are heart-based, they can generate immense cycles of this energy, but they find it hard to sustain."

At this point it became very difficult to receive the transmission. I'd noticed that sometimes weather systems affected transmission, but I really wanted to hear this, so I struggled to listen.

"Love flourishes when it is nurtured and cared for. When it is deemed useful and important, the love that's generated by the emerald ray of the heart chakra is extremely potent as a tool for healing individuals and the planet. This is more critical than the world realizes, because it is the surest conduit humans have to deity and Creator. It is also the surest route for prayers to be answered and for the individual to be able to make use of his/her own creative abilities as beings who share substance with the Great Source.

"You must teach the emerald frequency as a heart opener. Teach the heart opening sequence as a means to tap into Creator and all those who are sent to aid humanity. Teach the capacity to heal through love, to learn through love, to create through love.

Teach that forgiveness must be learned and practiced before love can flourish."

Forgiveness has never been easy for me. My Old Testament soul is more "eye for an eye" than "turn the other cheek" but I have since realized that we must forgive for our own sake, not the sake of the one who harmed us. Carrying resentments and anger lowers our own vibration, causes us untold pain and has no effect whatsoever on the one who caused the harm. It's a lose-lose place to get stuck in.

"You have seen that at times when you reach the Celestial frequency your heart chakra glows with an emerald radiance. At other times you access our energies, but the green grotto does not open. I will explain this now.

"Just as the Celestial frequency is one you now recognize and can therefore vibrate to, the green emerald frequency is one which makes it easier for earthlings to vibrate with love. As you know, the love frequency is a wavelength that not only accesses us but also allows the practitioner to utilize the celestial energies to heal and to accomplish other tasks. The emerald ray frequency is a different wavelength from the Celestial, but as it is easier to create while in an earth body, it is the frequency most teachers have their pupils use as Love. And it does radiate love –

however without the added frequency which few know, it cannot radiate the Celestial. Is this clear?"

I thought I understood the basic idea, so answered, "Mother, are you saying that the green frequency can accomplish healing and love, but it cannot necessarily utilize the Celestial to do other God-like accomplishments?"

"This is correct," she said. "Most of the Avatars and certain saints could do this well.

"To run both frequencies together is not easy for earthlings and must be trained. Work must also be done on the earth body from the Celestial, in order for it to hold the charge. The Emerald Heart frequency is the place to begin and will be explained in Book II.

Love for Humanity

"Love is gravely misunderstood on your planet, for it is often romantic love and sex that are equated with the term. The heart chakra is meant to be an all-encompassing love channel, one capable of great feats of healing and also capable of being used as a conduit to The Divine Intelligence. When love suffuses the individual, all life force of the entity, down to the cellular level and the soul level, is transformed. The bliss that is felt and catalogued by the intellect is reverberative throughout all fields of the being's electromagnetic self. Indeed, such love reverberates out into the world around the entity, sharing the frequency with those who are close at hand.

"When the entity is in the state of bliss, the way to God is easily achieved. The heart opens and the Divine Intelligence is available in ways not ordinarily so easily made use of. Yet it is seldom at that moment of such bliss that one thinks of God; rather in such times one thinks of the beloved.

"Yet, in truth, that same degree of bliss can be reached on behalf of fellow humans. When you love, you put aside judgments, do you not? So it is when forgiveness is invoked, or when a human loves another enough to put aside thoughts of self. The recipient of such love need not be only the "sweetheart," in your terms. The beloved may be one who is ill, or in need, or in need of forgiveness, or merely a passerby. The beloved may be the Planet Herself who is not only in need, but whose bounty is quite capable of conjuring bliss.

"When this bliss is reached, the heart chakra opens and generates the brilliant emerald frequency that you know well. When that frequency is being run, the channel to the Celestial opens dramatically and allows access. Visions come, prayers are clearly answered, clarity ensues and a sense of profound joy and fulfillment pervades the entity for a Divine

Connection has been made that carries on its frequency band the memory of Creator and of the times when the entity was in complete oneness with The Divine Source.

"The ecstatic visions of saints, the divine interventions in which humans took part, and the moment of supreme love between mortals, be they lovers, parents and children, or others loved in a specific set of circumstances, all these carried the waveband, the *frequency* of love.

"This frequency can be taught and learned. It can be better understood. It can be a pathway to God/Goddess/Creator for humanity to tread. It can change worlds and futures. But it must be taught quickly now.

"Love must be recognized on your plane for what it is... a vibrational frequency higher than the others, which has the power to transmute both energy and matter. The love frequency, when it is genuine, has the capacity to change your world, to eliminate war, hatred, corruption, abuse. To create in humans, and even in many of the other hybrids, a heightened sense of awareness of the cosmos and the connection mortals have to the great powers that exist.

"In the beginning," She said, "love was a given, because humankind had been part of Creator, Love was universal, love was all pervasive, love was *all* inclusive of the human, animal, vegetable, mineral kingdoms, all of which had been created to serve the higher good and to serve Creator.

"Love was everywhere. Love was the medium in which life existed. Then, there was a time of strife in heaven, as you term it. A time in which forces battled for supremacy... The strife was reflected, energetically, onto your planet and sides were taken up. It seems hard now for you to imagine that any would choose the Dark Side of the Fallen, but they, too, were powerful and many, and they were then, as they remain now, beautiful and seductive. The rewards they offered were manifold."

Power. Money. Sex. The rewards for being willing to live without conscience on the Dark Side have always been the same it seems, in every millennium since the dawn of time. And all it requires to receive all the world offers to satisfy greed is abandoning compassion, kindness, integrity, truth and love.

CHAPTER 19

The Emerald Heart Teaching

"The teaching today will be about the heart chakra and its emerald vibrations," the Mother said. "As you have seen, the heart has the capacity to act as a direct conduit into the hologram that is The Universe/God/The Central Sun. We have referred to it as the heart grotto in speaking to you because it appears to you often to be a great green cave out of which I emerge. This is acceptable as a human perception.

"The truth however is somewhat more complex. Certain frequencies carry on bands of color a direct conduit to the divine. In truth, each of the colors of the light spectrum reaches us in The Celestial, yet it is also true that the emerald ray of the heart is the most powerful and the most direct. It is also the most powerful opener, if you will, of direct communication.

"The great hologram of which you and all others are a part, vibrates at all speeds, all frequencies needless to say, but just as in plucking a particular string on a harp a specific note is called forth, so it is with the emerald chakra's ability to contact us directly and with immediacy.

"When the heart chakra is fully opened and attuned, a human or human/hybrid can, as you hypothesized, enter into the state of Avatar – one who can transmute matter and is no longer bound by what you believe to be the physical laws of nature.

"In truth, these laws themselves are merely hypotheses and human constructs, as is Time. Outside of your own consciousness these rules have no place nor power in the perception of other sentient races in the solar system or galaxy. They may be considered useful stepping stones, no more than that.

"So when you enter the heart grotto and find me there, and others as well if you so choose, you are immersed in the most loving and powerful vibration, one that can heal and pacify. It is important to your development now that you hold this vibration as long as possible each day.

"Why is forgiveness so important, Mother?" I asked. This was a concept I'd had a very hard time with because of a betrayal that had upended my life.

The answer was succinct.

"To carry hatred, rage, envy, anger, is the hardest burden of all on the heart. Forgiveness and the decision to simply let go if you cannot come to forgiveness, these are lessons hard for mortals but essential in order to do the work.

"If I were to rage at every injustice done to me, no life could be sustained on earth. So it is with humans. The heart grows and expands through forgiveness and contracts painfully, even atrophying, through these negative expressions of rage, envy, hatred, anger."

"As you have noticed, envy, anger, and a host of other human emotions prevent entry (to the heart grotto) by preventing your vibratory rate from being appropriate. Conversely, when you love deeply and consciously, the emerald energy expands exponentially and your powers with it.

"When you work as a healer, there is no judgment and no negotiating. Therefore the divine grace can be channeled through your hands without impediment. Were you to let ego or any negative emotion intrude, the divine substance evaporates and you are left with your own meager skills – meager by comparison, of course. Your body/mind provides an excellent conduit for this heart energy. Your heart is the best of you."

I tried to accept what she was saying and must have looked troubled because she added "this teaching is to help you understand that you must use your skills and your heart to alleviate suffering. Whether you do so by teaching, writing or laying on hands, you are an easy conduit for divine healing grace to enter the earth plane. Keep your heart chakra open and available to use for entry.

"You doubt yourself and in so doing you interfere with Our use of your gifts. This teaching is to help you understand that it is not you alone, but you as a conduit for Us, that heals. Be assured of this and therefore cease to fear and doubt.

"Love, forgiveness, sharing, truth, compassion, wisdom, open-mindedness, open-heartedness, justice, integrity, joy. Would the world not be a better place if these right thoughts and right actions superseded greed and violence? Find a way to preach this message in a new voice, a resonant voice. The world wishes to learn of energy and healing. These two are the key to making the message visible and desired."

CHAPTER 20

Sexuality

Having been taught about love on this cosmic level, I felt an immense need to understand the complexities of the male/female relationship as part of this love continuum, so sex seemed the next obvious issue to ask about. An intriguing answer came as The Mother talked of a dimensional shift in planetary energy that was triggered at that time. It seemed a non-sequiter at first, but turned out not to be one.

"The world is undergoing a dimensional shift," She said in answer to my query – she added that many great transformational planetary aspects will change the energetic face of the world over the next decade and a half. This shift (is) a beneficial one although many places in the world will feel its pressure in difficult ways. Humanity, in its current state of being is stubborn. It is easier to watch television than to think, easier to be subsumed by the electronic gadgetry that abounds than to serve the Gods and fellow humans. Easier to pursue money and luxury than to seek out the needs of those around you.

"Sexuality, too, is in a precarious state, for it grows detached from the heart chakra, and becomes merely another form of entertainment." *That* seemed to me a very significant statement. In the years since She made this statement, I've watched with increasing dismay as this "precarious state" has escalated radically.

"The first and second chakras are not meant to operate independently of the higher chakras. Profligacy and promiscuity cause (energy) depletion that drains the system of life-giving vital force. If humanity allows itself to be controlled by mindless sex and mindless electronic entertainment, it can easily be enslaved by forces on the planet that wish to keep the species in ignorance of its true potential.

"Sexuality is life force," She went on. "It has been subverted by religions, by tyrants of many sorts, some of which were barely recognizable as such. At its highest level, sexual lifeforce is the secret to long life and health. If males and females come together in truth and love, they can heal each other on a daily basis. The Chinese understand this energetic principle (with their vast understanding of Qi), but they fail the test of the heart chakra more often than not, understanding the power of the energies, but not the power of love."

"One of the truths we wish to have you speak is of the power of love and sexuality in proper balance," She told me. "You wonder how this can be as there is no such balance in your own life, but We tell you that it is coming to you."

That sounded comforting, but highly unlikely.

CHAPTER 21

The Nature of Time

The Nature of Time was explained in many ways by The Celestials in the years of their communication. I confess it wasn't easy to comprehend, even though I loved every bit of what they were saying and longed to know more. I understood what they were teaching on an intellectual level, but on a visceral level, the notion of multiple timelines wasn't easy to grasp and it was difficult for me to think of history as other than linear. I was told I had residual knowledge from time-out-of-mind when I had studied at the Time Monasteries in other incarnations and other dimensions, but if that was so, I had long ago forgotten most of it.

The only residual gift I seemed to have retained in this lifetime was that of Far Memory. They told me memory of all past lives and the lessons learned in them is stored in any current incarnation, in the hippocampuses of the brain, but is accessed only by a few in these current times.

The Best News

I loved everything about the study of Time... maybe because it's the one thing I can never get enough of. I was introduced to the Guardian of the Time Frequency, an extraordinary being, jovial, good-natured yet with considerable gravitas. He seemed happy to take an initiate on any journey in the annals of Time/Space, and he became for me a favorite teacher, so whether it was because of my previous learning in the Time Monasteries or because of his generosity and kindness, I enjoyed the information about the nature of Time more than any other subject I was shown.

I was told it's possible to learn to Time Jump. To consciously leave one time line and seek another, whether to recapture important knowledge or to alter perception of the experience. In an odd way, this Time Jumping is akin to certain kinds of psychotherapy, I think. It allows you to view what has been experienced, but mitigate the emotions that accompanied the experience. We can learn to alter our connection to Time to alleviate the pressure of an accelerating world, to alter our future and to even alter our past, by revisiting a traumatic incident and easing its distress. In some ways, meditation and other mind-quieting exercises do the same but the system They taught seemed to me more profound than any other I had experienced.

I hope to express all I've learned of the truth of Time in the next volume of this work, as it's part of the healing system I was told to teach, but I would like to offer a taste of it now as it seems so relevant to all our current lives.

CHAPTER 22

The Essence of Time

"You are in a time of bending and bendable time waves," said Vega, who very occasionally reappeared during my channeling sessions. His appearance often varied and he told me his people were Shape Shifters and could alter their appearance at will. "The time patterns you have grown accustomed to no longer apply. Earthlings have been kept in the dark, programmed endlessly with incorrect perceptions of reality. You are easily manipulated in your eagerness to serve gods you have been led to believe have your best interests at heart. This is often not the case.

"Time is not as you believe," he said. "Many have sought to mark its passing with graphs and clocks and charts, but *that* is not Time. Time is a dimension of reality that intersects with your own dimension. The wave that carries time perception – think of radio waves – is bending in on itself because of the photon belt radiation distortion. This is all according to The Plan and is not to be feared.

"This bending or distortion will affect all linear objects like computers, confusing them until the time when those intelligences learn to protect themselves and begin to evolve their own time consciousness. Think of it as a wrinkle in time's fabric, which allows distortion but also creates an interesting pattern of its own.

"Within this pattern new ideas and thoughts will emerge, including an observation of true time consciousness for those who can make that leap. As more people leap to time cognizance, more will be able to transition to space travel readiness. Off-world activity will take on a new and more plausible reality. Your species is primitive. Other species travel interdimensionally and intergalactically at the speed of light, the speed of thought, the speed of molecular energy. The speed of their zeal to be elsewhere.

"All this is hard to grasp but soon will not be."

I was intrigued, but wondered how it dovetailed with all else I was learning, and I needed practical advice on how to deal with time *now*. I asked if we can alter its passage with our minds.

"Most assuredly," I was told. "Even thinking of time shifts its molecular activity. Try today to suspend disbelief for a day – believe that you can speed time up or slow it down. See what happens and return tonight with your report. Then we will speak further."

Try it for yourself – you may be startled by the results as I was indeed startled by my experiments. When we spoke again, there was more information.

"Time is compressing," Vega said. "You and others feel the discomforts of this pressure."

"Why is time compressing?" I asked.

"The end times of great cycles cause compression," he said without elaborating. I assured he was speaking of the 25,865 year cycle The Mother had spoken of.

"You must remember time is an abstraction but one with a certain cosmic substance. It is neither linear nor spiral nor even quite the arcing wave band that Einstein hypothesized, although that construct is useful at your planet's level of development. As I once told you, time (for an individual) emanates from your center, radiating out in an infinite number of beams or time lines. Not all timelines will you follow, although at times one may be on several time lines simultaneously. You might say that time is linear, circular, spiral, waved *and* a continuum all at once – it is flexible and malleable with infinite capacity to change, wrinkle, fold in on itself and perform other anomalous feats because of its atomic structure. I use the word atomic loosely, as you have as yet no word in your language for the structure of time's substance. Suffice to say you may bend it to your needs. We will cause you to remember your training from other mystery schools so you may do this." What mystery schools? Where and when had I been trained? I wondered if the fact that I'd never been able to wear a watch successfully, because they were never accurate once I wore them, had something to do with my relationship to time. I did seem to have an odd gift for always knowing what time it is, even without a watch.

"Time is quite 'plastic' now," he continued. "It expands and contracts, even seems to stop at whim. You find this disconcerting, but once you get the hang of it, you will find it liberating. You are not meant to be constrained by time as you have been. You have watched the Mother breathe. Do you think that was seen in ordinary time? It was not. You have fought on battlefields alongside angels, while your earth body engaged in sleep. Again, not ordinary time. You have been taken to other places to be taught. Not in ordinary time. Do you begin to understand? Do you wish to pursue time as a topic?" Vega asked and of course, I said yes.

"You must understand that in order to travel appropriately in space, you must be able to bend time and transmute the wave to your need," he said.

"I hear you," I answered, "but that's hard to grasp."

Vega said gently, "Imagine a giant ribbon of minute particles that traverse space in an almost endless band. Now imagine an infinite number of such ribbons capable of interweaving and intersecting molecularly with each other. That is Time."

"That's a nice image," I said, "but how does that image apply to a life?"

"Each life generates many time ribbons. Sometimes vast numbers. The consciousness for the most part permits itself to follow one ribbon. Sometimes it allows several, as when you, Alana, unfold a past life from the cellular storage facility in your brain. Thus you can be Catherine living in New York or Connecticut on one ribbon, but suddenly you are another on a Celtic battlefield, and each life is running with clarity for you. This is why you sometimes speak of the kaleidoscope of lives clicking in, or feel awash in a wave of *other* remembrance.

When that happens you are no less yourself. Rather you are more than yourself."

"Wow!" I said, finally *getting* how my psychic Far-Memory worked. It was a mystery that had so often helped me in writing historical fiction, I'd come to rely on it without questioning.

"Wow, indeed," Vega said matter-of-factly, then added, "You were thinking for a moment on The Great Mysteries. Time is not one, precisely. It will be understood by your scientists in the next generation and by most of humanity in times to come."

"What must we do now with this knowledge?" I asked perplexed.

"Stay alert," he answered. "Listen with these expanded senses. Choose for yourself. Use your (Time) power to create – to spread the word and to make your life easier. Chasing your tail keeps you from doing your (spiritual) work, so many forces have worked to immobilize you in this manner.

"You (humans) are being given help by certain factions now," he said, "and you are expanding your consciousness to contain larger ideas, closer to the truth. Your vistas enlarge cosmically, and your doorways are opening. Native people will help you in certain ways. Be open to their teaching when it can be obtained." He was so right about this. My Indian friends are infinitely more in touch with the cosmos and with the reality of time. As I worked with Native teachers, much of what I was being told took on a more understandable dimension.

But Vega also added a warning. There were dark forces that also know the secret of Time Jumping and have used it for evil purpose.

"These time jumpers are farther along in their knowledge of how time/space functions. They use an accelerator particle technology based on Nikola Tesla's design that alters the time wave, making it unstable and permeable. When they do this now, information can be electrically introduced into the field. It is as if a computer expert interjects new data onto/into an existing program. When this happens, changes occur.

"The agendas vary and the results vary. This is different from the concept of probable timelines and parallel lifetimes (as I had been shown it) because it is artificially induced.

"It is beyond your ability to influence, but not beyond *our* ability, should we choose to interfere. Our prime directive has been the unfoldment of the human species and its galactic hybrids, so interference has not been necessary (in the matter of Time). But if they endanger the planet's total molecular integrity, we will intercede.

"Many are being given this information, so the knowledge of what transpires is not lost. We are aware that you do not yet know how to disseminate this, but the time comes soon to know."

The Mother voice chimed in unexpectedly.

"You are to write of Time," She said authoritatively. "The concept of Time as you know it was a palliative one implanted in your (human's) psyches to control you. Slaves work to Time constraints, Gods do not. Nonetheless, the concept itself proves useful to you but you must not allow yourself to be enslaved as time escalates. As the frequencies become more challenging and you vibrate higher and higher in the internal worlds, the temptation is to run faster and faster in your external world, trying to catch up. This is of course impossible, but it is done as a factor of confusion about the true Time Nature of reality."

Vega said there was a new timeline in progress for planet Earth.

"Those on the new timeline will start to see massive change in their own worlds. Different friends, needs, food, drink, desires, work, ideas, opportunities. Doors swinging open, money coming in (from new sources), challenges falling away." He said many were having a new chakra opened in their energy fields so they could accelerate appropriately.

"Those with the High Heart opened (a new aqua colored chakra located between the heart and throat chakras, slightly to the left of center) will be able to communicate newly and with other realms (telepathically). Time goes faster and higher. The vibration is more refined.

"There are physical needs to meet the new vibration – exercise, water, air, movement, Qi Gong and Truth work. The rewards will multiply quickly.

"Humans must learn to keep vibrating at the Celestial rate all day long. They will hold this (vibration) for longer and longer periods. Soon it will be second nature."

"Your timeline is accelerated, as you know. Everyone on your planet is aware to some degree. Years feel shorter, days feel fleeting. Christmas will be upon you and you will barely feel prepared. This was not the case in more leisurely decades.

"Time expands and contracts in waves of energy particles. But what you perceive is not that – you feel the tug of timelines that hold you to the linear past.

"Soon the future will tug as hard, and you will feel pulled wildly by it. We will train you to time jump and to time scan. You have had this ability in times past and can easily access it now. The year 2000 was a line of demarcation on a larger (Cosmic) Timeline. It marked a rite of passage into understanding. Certainly for you and for many."

I was told 2012 would provide another such leap of consciousness for us all, but not the end of the world, despite the fact that many people in the spiritual movement thought December 21st, 2012 – the end date of the Mayan Calendar – heralded the end. I asked for clarification about that.

The Mothers said the planet Herself will not be destroyed anytime soon. The planet, it seems, occupies too important a place in the Cosmic scheme of things for those in charge to allow its destruction. Unfortunately for us, it seems we humans are quite capable of instigating *our* own destruction as a species. In fact, She said, if humanity chooses the low road, much of our species may be decimated in order to protect the planet itself from our follies. Remember the "ants from a picnic blanket" analogy?

She said the energies would escalate exponentially from 2012 to 2015.

PART V

Conclusion for Now

Conclusion: It's Not Too Late

I believe we are being sent a Message to the Heart of the World from the Heart of the Cosmos. The Mothers are giving us a roadmap for changing the future of humanity and our planet and the message seems to include the comforting idea that this time, they don't want us to fail. They're saying that with Divine help we can succeed beyond our wildest dreams, reach 4th and 5th Dimensional Consciousness and enter the prophesied Golden Age, provided we find a way to stem the tide of greed and corruption that has subsumed our country and much of the world.

What exactly can we humans do to turn the tide? What can we seemingly powerless, flawed, frail, struggling millions do that could possibly make the slightest difference to the mega-rich, mega-greedy, legally empowered giants – corporate, governmental and individual – that have set us on this collision course for disaster?

When I asked that question of the Mothers, the answer was simple and immediate:

"One human at a time. One act at a time. One decision at a time. If each who cares to raise himself or herself and to raise your civilization's promise, makes a commitment to the heart-centered path of love, compassion, forgiveness, the Groundswell will begin to spread like a tincture. One drop of poison can contaminate a reservoir, but a single drop of love or decency can change the molecular structure of the energy of the world. A poet of Earth* was once inspired to write, 'Even in times of darkness, that is the time to love. That an act of love may tip the balance.'

"Thus, it is now as it has always been, a choice made by humans as to whom and what they will become."

The Mothers asserted over and over again that the way to conquer the seemingly invincible greed, power-madness, destructiveness and human-to-human disconnection that plagues our planet, and to thwart the control that the Powerful seek to exercise over the rest of humanity, is by reinforcing humanity's best uniqueness, its great and courageous heart.

They stressed that the InterWebs would become our means of spreading Truths, of uncovering long buried secrets and lies, of re-establishing the power of the people over the power of the rich and ruthless. They said that words and the internet would be our means of touching each other's consciousness and hearts in times of terrible dangers to come. A means to utilize the strength of a universal outpouring of knowledge, emotion, and dynamic energy to build a better world, hand to hand and heart to heart, beyond the ordinary boundaries of time/space. A way to keep humanity from becoming completely controlled by those whose political and financial power seems overwhelming and unbeatable, so that we can once again realize the magnitude of our own strength and power as a united species.

Alone we're powerless. Together, there are more of us who wish to build than to destroy. We humans have done it before – built civilizations from scratch – against the odds and the will of the powerful.

What if with the Mothers' help we can do it this time?

*Rainer Maria Rilke

The Message Continues

This book is just the tip of the iceberg. Because so much information was channeled I've divided it into segments.

I hope to make Book Two available before 2014 is over. Book Two will explore what The Mothers taught about the frequencies of light and sound as a means to heal ourselves and our homeworld and will explain in detail the Emerald Heart Frequency. If you would like to be alerted about its publication date, please contact me on my website:

www.CathyCashSpellman.com.

Cathy Cash Spellman is the author of five New York Times and International Bestsellers. Her books have been sold in 22 countries, and her novel *Bless the Child* was a Paramount movie.

www.ingramcontent.com/pod-product-compliance
Lightning Source LLC
Chambersburg PA
CBHW031640040426
42453CB00006B/169